SHE CALLED ME DAD

She Called Me Dad

HOPE FOR RELATIONSHIP IN A WOUNDED WORLD

Joseph Tosini

CITYHILL PUBLISHING
Columbia, Missouri

ISBN   0-939159-20-1

Scripture quotations are taken from the Holy Bible, New International Version. Copyright © 1973, 1978, 1984 International Bible Society. Used by permission.

Printed in the U.S.A.
Cityhill Publishing
4600 Christian Fellowship Road
Columbia, MO U.S.A. 65203

DEDICATION

This book is dedicated to my dad, the person who has given me more than anyone else, letting me observe his strengths while sharing with me the depth of his humanity. His passing has left a hole in my heart that cannot be filled; his memory is a treasure I would never exchange.

Other books by Joseph Tosini

Is There Not A Cause? Beyond the Disappointment of Aimless Christianity

Is There Not A Cause? Study Guide

CONTENTS

THANKS

This manuscript does not list by name a cast of characters vital to this story, and to do them justice would take another book. They are the friends and family members whose unconditional love and support provided me the security and strength to reach out to Heidi and invite her not only into my life, but into theirs as well.

Thank you, Holly, for allowing me a parental place in Heidi's life that I do not deserve.

To my brother John and my sister Marybeth, along with their spouses, Michelle and Randy: Thank you for not just accepting Heidi, but making her feel part of you instantly and continuing to do so.

To my parents, who couldn't have been more supportive; their love to Heidi and forgiveness to me speaks volumes in understanding God's heart toward his children.

As in our first book, *Is There Not A Cause?*, the producing of this manuscript was a team effort, and once again the team rose to the occasion under some stressful circumstances.

Jan Petersen, who designed the book, suffered the loss of her mother. Bob Briggs, our chief editor, had his fifth child during deadline week.

Special thanks to Ann Weaver, whose heart, home, and service is always available without restraint. She filled in all the gaps and did a great job. And, as usual, the rest of the team—Dick, Betty, Jan, Debbie, Pam, Sherry, and Frank— were called upon to go the extra mile. Thank you.

To a great church that rejoices and weeps together: Well done.

And finally, Dawn, Jodi, and Joy, you have made this story possible.

SECTION ONE:

SEPARATE NO MORE

PROLOGUE

Through the week, her excitement grew about her idea. Her mother had gotten married just months before. This would be the ideal opportunity to let the man know she was glad he had entered her life. With no prompting from her mom, she found the proper aisle at the grocery store and searched through the stacks for that one special card she hoped would please him.

The man and the little girl had fun before, when he just came over for a few hours in the evenings and on weekends. But since the three had moved in together, things were different. Evening television shows left no time to play together; he never seemed to have much to talk with her about.

Maybe the card would change things.

When the special day arrived, she stepped silently into the kitchen, interrupting the man's conversation by reaching out and handing him a sealed white envelope. Her eyes searched the floor, waiting for the seconds to elapse.

The little girl hadn't known how to tell anyone about her hopes. Maybe this card would convey the message that she would welcome him into a more special role in her life. Maybe he would then begin to fill the gap that made her different from all her friends. She imagined being closer, meaning more to him. But she was afraid.

Resuming his discussion with the little girl's mother, he tore at the paper. He glanced momentarily at the card's front, then pulled the flap open.

Written in the fluttering handwriting of a young girl just learning cursive were the words, "Happy Father's Day."

Shifting her wide eyes up toward him and risking a shy smile, the little girl waited silently. She had ventured into a dream where strong arms wrapped gently around her, warming the cold loneliness deep inside.

But suddenly, his face darted away from the card—and away from her.

"I'm not your father," he snapped, dropping the card on the table like so much junk mail.

The little girl stood paralyzed. With her eyes fixed in a trance-like stare, the heat of her humiliation seared a message on her heart. Never again would she dare to dream of a father. Never again, vowed this little girl named Heidi, would she call a man "Dad."

*T*ILDEN PARK

Holly had grown distant. We had been together for several months, sharing the "good life" of Berkeley, California, at the height of the '60s. I didn't know why she had changed; another boyfriend probably.

"Let's go for a drive," she said.

We headed to Tilden Park. Colorful rose gardens bordered the road on one side, and a panoramic view of the bay opened up in the other direction. The Golden Gate and the Oakland Bay bridges lined the distant landscape.

Visiting this park had always been enjoyable, but this day was different. Tension hung in the air. With no conversation to penetrate the silence, I grew more uneasy. My mind rehearsed the relationship-ending statement I expected to hear. "It's been fun, but . . ." or some variation on that theme.

Still with no words, I stopped the car near the meadow area where we had often come. We sat down in the grass. I looked at Holly, then away, allowing her to choose the moment to begin. Finally, from behind a distant stare, she offered her announcement.

"I'm pregnant," she said, slamming through the silence.

The words stung me. In one short moment they crashed through every insulating layer of my mind. A damp coolness infected my hands. Panic started like a brushfire in my mind.

"Are you sure?" I asked, desperately searching for a reason to reject the unthinkable.

"Yes, I'm sure," she said coolly, not breaking her gaze into the distance.

"Are you sure it's me?" I asked. A slight stammer now overshadowed my ordinarily cocky and carefree demeanor. It was my last-ditch effort to escape the net that was snaring me. Holly shot back a disgusted look, resenting the implications.

"Of course it's you."

It had never occurred to me this could happen; I assumed she had been taking precautions to make sure our few months together wouldn't produce a pregnancy.

"Do you want to get an abortion?" I asked.

"No," she replied without hesitation.

"What do you want to do?" I asked, trying to match Holly's sense of calm.

"I'm going to go to the East Coast and have this child," she said decisively, "and start a new life." Clearly, she had already weighed her options and set her course. Where would I fit in, I wondered.

"Do you want to get married?" I asked. She glanced over at me and laughed. It was quiet for a few minutes. As the panic subsided, I pondered the possibilities.

"What do you want me to do?" I asked, feeling like an outsider peeking into someone else's choices.

"I just need money to help with the trip back to the East Coast," Holly replied.

Despite its search, my mind produced no solutions. I felt like I was walking off a plank. I couldn't turn around, couldn't step aside. Finally, I offered the only words that seemed to fit the moment. "I'm sorry."

Holly drew in her distant gaze and concluded the conversation with a measure of warmth. "So am I."

FAREWELL

I drove Holly to the San Francisco airport, where we said our last good-byes. To get money for the trip, we had written some bad checks and cashed them at liquor stores. We called it our Bonnie and Clyde routine.

As I waved good-bye and watched the plane pull away from the gate, I began pondering the events that had led to this parting, trying to make sense of the confusion that had settled upon me. It had been less than two years since I had left New York . . . .

Inside me, a frustration was mounting, pushing its way out, a tension between what was and what ought to be. My world wasn't the idyllic place portrayed on the Ozzie and Harriet show. Home for most of my growing-up years had been a working class neighborhood in Brooklyn, a crowded cluster of row houses and apartment buildings where people saw each other for who they were. There were no sprawling lawns, hedges, or privacy fences to shelter personal lives from a neighbor's view. When arguments broke out, the walls and ceilings didn't stop the sound. There was no hiding it when somebody came home tottering drunk. On the street, truck drivers would cuss each other out, jump out in the middle of traffic, and start swinging. I saw legless old men panhandling pencils and watched evicted tenants despairing as the authorities plopped their furniture out onto the street.

Though I wasn't outwardly philosophical, growing up where I did, I couldn't help thinking about life. The world didn't make much sense. My choice in music reflected the tensions of the time: songs by Bob Dylan; Janis Joplin; Peter, Paul & Mary; Richie Havens. My friends weren't the cheerleaders and class presidents who seemed to live in a plastic world, but those who had a non-conformist bent. Most were cynics like me who thought much of what people made out to be important was really a big joke.

Some friends of mine had already been sent to Vietnam, and my draft number made it clear I was a prime candidate. I was ready to make a break from my New York roots, but Southeast Asia was definitely not my idea of a good time.

My friend George and I went to sign up for the draft, as required, and in my own form of protest, I turned the affair into a comic routine. Just outside the office, I got down on my knees and crawled through the door, feigning some strange and severe handicap. "You're supposed to come here when you're eighteen," I told the clerk at the desk, who was giving me a curious stare. "But I'm not really sure of my age. You see, I've got some serious problems." As an employee filled out a medical form and ran down a standard list of questions, I gave her every reason I could think of to disqualify me from the draft.

"Your parents' names?"

"I'm an orphan, ma'am. Raised my brothers and sisters by myself. It's a sad story. I'll have to tell you about it. I've spent most of my life as an emotional cripple."

"Your address, please?"

"Well, we're on the go a lot. My family travels with the Ringling Brothers circus. My father's a midget, and my mother is the fat lady in the freak show."

"What color are your eyes?"

"They change all the time. It's part of that terminal disease I was telling you about."

She had me step on the scale. "A hundred and ninety pounds?" I exclaimed. "You're kidding! I've lost another twenty pounds? It must be that tapeworm. You know, even so I just can't stop eating. It would cost a fortune for the army to feed me."

"No, ma'am, you sure don't want me in Vietnam. Not with all my problems." My friend was in hysterics. The clerk told me I had a future as a stand-up comic. By then, the commotion had attracted the attention of a supervisor who had heard the woman ask me to sign my name. Pretending to be illiterate, at the bottom of the form I scrawled a crude X. That was the last straw. The supervisor shut down the sideshow, leaving us with some choice words to ponder on our way out.

College would have kept me out of the draft, but the one semester I had already sat in class proved to be a waste. I was shooting pool more than studying. But as I thought about my options, the idea of learning to be an airline pilot excited me. Besides, aeronautics school would keep me out of the draft.

I found a good flight school on the West Coast. I welcomed the chance to leave the familiar behind and plunge into the center of the social revolution. What better place to go in 1967 than California where the countercultural crescendo was reaching its height. . . .

As I stood watching Holly's plane taxi toward the runway, the rhetoric about an age of "harmony and understanding" was not making much sense. The California dream, for me anyway, had become a nightmare. When I had left New York, I was an eighteen-year-old kid anticipating joining a throng of people who had found a new kind of freedom. But my carefree pursuits seemed to have produced a trail of devastation. The fun I'd had paled in comparison to the despair that was settling over me.

It was an odd mixture of feelings stirring inside. On the one hand, I felt some relief. One burden would be gone: Holly wanted nothing to do with me. Away from that airport terminal rolled the complications of a relationship that had run dry. But amid all the thoughts and questions about my days in California, one realization swept through me like the chilling gust of an approaching thunderstorm. I was saying good-bye to someone who would soon give birth to a baby—a new human life for which I was responsible.

As I stood recounting my California life, I felt so foolish, like an overconfident preschooler who spills a big glass of milk. I wasn't even twenty years old yet, and I was still trying to make sense of my life. I didn't feel prepared to be an adult, let alone a parent.

Yet I felt a deep-seated responsibility for that child. Instinctively, I knew the feeling would never diminish. I was stinging from the pain. The few months' pleasure I had enjoyed with Holly would be far outweighed by years of regret, a lingering ache that I would have to keep hidden in a dim corner of my private world.

I tried to tell myself that Holly would be better off without me. She's responsible and independent. She'll do well on her own. She's young, attractive, I told myself. No doubt she'll find the ideal husband, someone far more qualified for fatherhood than I—a lawyer, perhaps—who will embrace the child as his own. The child would have a good home, a family, and a stand-in father with whom the child would be perfectly satisfied. Maybe Holly's decision to leave is for the best, I thought.

My mind drifted to my own father. What would he say if he knew? I thought about how much he had invested in me, how he had sacrificed for my sake, and had left me with a deep sense of security. My first brush with fatherhood wasn't matching up very well to the family values he had displayed over the course of my life.

I thought back to the time I had said good-bye to my father in New York late in the spring of 1967 . . . .

On the day I was to leave, I threw my bags into my father's car, and we drove to an auto repair shop where I picked up the car that I would drive West, a 1966 mountain green Corvette. I had arranged for some work to be done to make it road ready.

As we finished our business and prepared to say good-bye, my excitement produced an enthusiastic smile. At last I was heading for California. But then I noticed on the cheeks beneath my father's sunglasses a streak of tears. The last time I had seen him cry was thirteen years before, when his best friend, my godfather, had died.

I was taken aback by his emotion. My eighteen-year-old mind offered only promises of a thrilling tomorrow. My father's perspective was clearly different. It wasn't that he would prevent me from going, despite the pressure from the rest of the clan to keep every family member huddled within shouting range of the Statue of Liberty. But I was his first child, the first to leave, and he seemed pained by the prospect of separation. Perhaps he saw a boy unprepared for the disappointments that undoubtedly lay ahead.

My father knew my thoughts and feelings; he knew I was looking for something that would take me away. I figured I was just going out to California for awhile; I didn't see how significant a change this would be. From now on, home would be a place for me to visit. This is a tough thing for my father, I thought.

"Take care of yourself," he said. "And call if you have any problems." He slipped me a one hundred dollar bill. "I love you." He hugged me and kissed my cheek.

"I love you, too," I said.

Off I went. Ordinarily I would have switched on the radio in that new Corvette and blasted the music loud enough to drive out any other thoughts. But this day, as I drove off and glanced in the rear view mirror to catch a final glimpse of my father, I left the knob alone. Why the tears, I wondered?

As I pondered his display of emotion, I thought back on the way he had raised me. Despite the responsibilities he had shouldered, he had always made time for me.

My father opened up a television repair business just as televisions came on the market. He worked a grueling schedule six days a week, opening the door at 9 a.m. and staying until he turned off the lights at 9 p.m. But every evening at 5 o'clock, I could count on him coming home for dinner and, no matter how tired he was, he would grab a mitt and play ball with me. He rarely missed a little league game; what a thrill it had been to look up in the stands and see my dad pulling for me.

It wasn't that he was some kind of saint or superstar, I thought as the New York skyline faded behind me. He had made mistakes, gotten angry, spoken cross words to my mother. He was neither a perfect person nor a perfect father. But in our years together, somehow he had demonstrated that I was significant to him. He hadn't spent countless hours with me or read bedtime stories to me every night. I just knew that in the midst of his pressures, he had extended himself for me. My welfare had been his utmost concern.

This farewell marked a significant transition in our relationship. No longer would my parents be the dominant people in my life. Now would come my chance to make my own decisions and explore my own values. I would take what I had been given by my father and begin building my own life. . . .

How disappointed he would be, I thought, leaning against the airport railing. His commitment and sacrifice had provided security for his children. What would he think if he found out I was responsible for bringing a life into the world but wouldn't fill the role of father?

CALIFORNIA DREAMIN'

Holly's plane was gone now. Another airliner had taxied to the gate to take its place. There was no reason for me to stay, but somehow I wasn't ready to go. As people scurried around to meet the arriving passengers, I kept staring out the terminal window, watching the planes take off and land.

My world was disintegrating like a sand castle overtaken by the tide. I was just a little over two years out of high school and in total despair. Why was everyone around me getting hurt? Every direction I looked there was tragedy that I had some part in. It's not that I was trying to do anybody wrong, but I couldn't control the forces my choices had set in motion.

How had things changed so quickly? How had this era of my life, which had begun with such promise, dissolved into such hopelessness? I thought back on my reckless entry into my California dream . . . .

I settled into my breezy, two-seater convertible and sped westward on the fast and open lanes of the cross-country freeways. By the time I was ready to pull off the road for a night, the signs were announcing Des Moines, Iowa. I was more than one thousand miles from home, several states farther west than I'd ever been. Spreading out my sleeping bag in a field—the lodging style in vogue with my crowd—I bedded down. No motel for this travelin' man.

The next morning, though, I discovered that I'd camped in unfriendly territory. My one-night bedroom turned out to be near a swamp where millions of mosquitoes made their home. Hundreds of them had personally welcomed me to the Midwest; they sent me straight to the hospital where I begged for something to keep the itching and swelling down.

The bug battle slowed me down some, but it didn't squelch my enthusiasm for this adventure. I could pick up the speed in my automobile, and every turn of the road brought something I'd never seen before. Heading through Wyoming, I was awed by the open expanse. Crowded streets, neon lights, and steel skyscrapers had been my world for eighteen years. Now windswept wheat fields and sage brush prairies seemed to stretch with the miles, ever pushing back the jagged mountains on the horizon. By night, the broad sky overwhelmed me with the lights of a thousand galaxies. Life seemed full, and the farther west I drove the more adrenaline surged as I anticipated what might await me on the coast.

In the middle of Utah, with the fuel gauge dropping, I made a quick decision to pull off for gas. The Corvette's speedometer had been topping 120—there were no speed limits posted out West to keep me down—when I spotted a station. Shifting down, I whipped toward the pumps. An attendant standing nearby looked up, startled. With sudden terror, he began waving his arms wildly to slow me. My foot smashed the brakes in reply, but the Corvette kept skidding past the pumps, laying down two long black lines of rubber in its path.

"Hey, I'm sorry," I said, after backing up. "I've been driving so long on this road I didn't realize how fast I was going." He shook his head, looking at me like I was a discharged mental patient. And so I came, with my tires squealing, steering my way into the California dream.

Arriving in the San Francisco Bay area, I pulled into the apartment complex where the flight school had placed me. Looking around, I could tell immediately this was no family housing unit. Mostly single and in their twenties, these people looked and talked like they wanted to pack every day with twenty-four hours of good times.

It wasn't even dark yet on my first day in California before somebody invited me to a party. It would be that night at the complex to welcome the new residents. "I'm not even unpacked yet, and the party's begun," I thought. "This is the life!"

At the party, my eastern accent got the attention of the big Hawaiian bartender. He was intrigued that I was from New York. Looking around, I spotted a young woman playing pool. Her skin-tight miniskirt documented her every move and hid only a few inches of her long legs.

The bartender quickly tuned in to my wavelength and started speculating about my chances of getting her attention. I wasn't the only guy in the place eyeing the main attraction.

"Let the New York City boy play," he said, pointing toward the pool table, giving me an edge on the onlooking California competition. He wondered how far my cocky routine would carry me.

"C'mon. You want to play me?" the woman asked, bending over to rack up the balls.

This woman, who turned out to be an airline flight attendant, shot a strong game of pool, attracting a sea of silent stares every time she leaned over to gauge a shot. I, of course, was earning the envy of every guy in the place.

"Where are you from?" she said, opening the conversation.

"New York," I said. That seemed to intrigue her, along with my Brooklyn accent. The dream seemed to be off to a good start, I thought to myself, glancing around at some of the onlookers.

When I sank the last ball, I looked up with a little smirk. My bartender friend, who had been rewarding my efforts with boiler-maker after boilermaker, nodded with approval. He was proud of his adopted New York boy.

With phase one complete, I made the next move. "Do you want to dance?" I asked.

"Sure," she said.

By this time I was loosening up, getting right into the flow of the party. And my wise guy instincts were kicking in—with a little help from the liquor.

"Can you dance any better than you can play pool?" I said, chiding her with my taunting grin.

Flaring her nostrils at my wise crack and breaking into a little grin of her own, she grabbed my hand and started dragging me toward the dance floor. "Let's find out," she said.

We shared a few more dances. Eventually, though, she wandered back to the pool table.

I ended up back at the bar where my 260-pound friend helped me out with another drink. Glancing over toward the entryway, I noticed a striking young woman making her entrance. Every head in the place turned. In had walked a tall, shapely blonde clad only in short blue jean cutoffs and a skimpy wrap-around top. Her gait was confident; she seemed accustomed to the stares. A real California girl, I thought.

The bartender motioned for me to lean over close to him.

"She's been in *Playboy*," he told me.

"Come on," I said, assuming he was setting me up.

"I'm not kidding," he assured me. His silent look issued the challenge. How would his Brooklyn boy do with the cream of the California crop?

By this time, the boilermakers had added ample boldness to my natural style.

"This is Joe from New York," the bartender said, gesturing toward me. That was all I needed. After a brief interaction, we ended up on the dance floor. "Were you really in *Playboy*?" I asked after a few minutes. She laughed, throwing her blond hair back, seeming to welcome the attention.

"What do you think?" she asked, keeping me guessing.

After a few minutes, a few dances and a few more stops at the bar, we sat down on a nearby couch. She settled onto my lap; my arms found their way around her and pulled her toward me.

What a place, I thought. I just got here and look at me. I'm the youngest guy here, and I stepped right in and took over. I love it! California, here I am!

Suddenly, the dream was interrupted. I guess I'd had one drink—and one dance—too many. The room seemed to be spinning slowly; my eyes lost their focus. Nausea spilled through me. This alleged pin-up had me pinned to the couch, and as I suddenly tried to pull away—

"Blggghhhhuuuhhgggh." I threw up—right down her blouse.

The cool New York routine was over. She pulled away rather abruptly. I was too drunk to be overly embarrassed, and I stumbled out, trying to salvage what dignity I could and make my exit as graciously as possible. Unfortunately, the swimming pool got in my way. I fell in. The cold water sobered me enough that I found my way home.

The next morning I woke up on the floor between the two single beds. The lamp was knocked over; the pillows and covers were off the beds; my dripping clothes were strewn about. Rubbing my head, I was trying to reconstruct the events of the previous night when the telephone rang.

"Joseph? How's it going out there?" It was my mother. She was keeping a promise to call me as soon as I arrived.

"Fine, Mom. Yeah, things are goin' just fine," I said, grimacing from a throbbing headache and noticing that my room looked like it had been ransacked.

My California dream was underway. . . .

I smiled to myself, remembering these events from over a year before. But now confusion had evaporated the glamor of my new adventure. Life wasn't turning out as I had expected. How had this happened, I continued to wonder. How had I come to be standing here, saying good-bye to someone it seemed like I hardly knew who was carrying a child I had fathered?

I turned from the railing, thrust my hands into my pockets, and began walking slowly through the terminal, thinking back on the few months I had shared with Holly and the lifestyle I had settled into. . . .

Three doors down from the apartment I was living in, a sharp, sophisticated looking woman, usually dressed in business-type skirts or dresses, had come in and out of an apartment several times over the last weeks. Sometimes if I was leaning against the railing on the balcony, I would look over as she approached the steps leading up to our apartments and nod hello as she walked past. She was polite but distant, nodding with a brief smile in return.

My roommates were planning on having some friends over for a party one night, and when I saw this woman arriving home from work, I asked if she would like to join us.

"There are some people coming over tonight," I said. "Do you want to come?"

"Sounds fine," said the woman, whose name was Holly. "I'll be there."

She surprised me when I saw her walk in that night. Leaving her professional image behind, she strode in wearing blue jeans and a T-shirt, looking much more like my other friends than she normally did.

After the round of introductions, she surprised me again. As usual, people were sitting around on the floor, listening to music, munching on chips, and sipping sangria. One of my friends passed some marijuana to Holly. I looked to see what she would do. She didn't hesitate; she brought the joint up to her lips and took a deep drag. I had misread this girl, I thought. But then she had kept relatively quiet, not giving me much to go on. "I'm really surprised you're doing this," I told her.

She responded with an elusive smile, which I took as an invitation. After a few joints and a few more glasses of sangria, it was easy to break through the awkwardness and act on our mutual attraction. Something clicked between us.

Before saying good night, we agreed to get together again. We would play tennis later that week.

Several months later, we had the idea of heading to Mexico for a few days. We could sleep on the beach, we decided, imagining warm, serene nights with stars filling the sky and the rhythmic sound of waves tumbling ashore. When we got down to Ensenada, though, we grew worried. We seemed to be the main attraction as we rolled into town in the Corvette. We could get killed in our sleep, we thought. Besides, it looked like rain, so we headed back toward the border to find a motel.

"I need a room for two," I told the motel clerk, fidgeting a bit. I didn't know if he would ask whether we were married, and I didn't know what I would say if he did. But he just shoved the registration forms toward me and handed me a key.

Holly never blended in much with the other people who became my friends in California. Despite her contact with me, she maintained a distance from the countercultural lifestyle I had plunged into.

Her apartment, for instance, was tastefully decorated with pictures, curtains, and dining room furniture, as was fitting of a more conservative, responsible type. In our place, though, furniture was never hip. We just threw down mattresses for beds and laid out big pillows for chairs. Sheets seemed to work fine as curtains. For meals, we sat cross legged on the living room floor and ate with chopsticks.

At nearly every meal, some dish was seasoned with marijuana, and marijuana brownies were always the dessert of choice. Our place became the hub of a continual party. Day or night, somebody was high or getting high. After a while, smoking pot got to be as routine as drinking water.

My roommate John and I decided we were going to stay high for six weeks, so I skipped a session of flight school to accommodate our experiment. We would get crazy together; lying with our backs on the floor, we would do the "turtle" dance, circling our hands and legs in the air. John made good on his vow to wear the same pair of jeans the whole time—even when he slept. As he smoked a joint or a cigarette he'd flick the ashes on his pants, get this self-congratulatory grin on his face, and rub the powder into the fabric.

Our third roommate, Doug, and I had first introduced John to the world of drugs, thinking we were inviting him into an exciting new dimension of mind-expanding experiences. But as the months went by, John stepped well beyond our partying patterns. In addition to our steady diet of marijuana, he started using LSD regularly and experimenting with an array of other hard drugs.

One night, he was hallucinating heavily and started to lose control. For more than an hour, John sat fully clothed in the bathtub of our apartment, while his ravaged mind betrayed him. All I could do was sit with him and wait, while he fought to escape his isolated world of relentless terror. I kept telling him everything would be all right, though I wasn't sure it would be.

This was California dreamin'? That night, after watching John's frightening mind journey, my drug desire started to wane. I started wondering where this was all going to lead.

Doug, a Vietnam veteran in his mid-twenties, had a job building cars at a General Motors plant. He wanted to collect some fast cash so he could quit his job and finance a year of scuba diving school. He ventured into the drug trade with his co-workers on the assembly line. Traffic through the apartment picked up as suppliers made their drops and buyers picked up their product. People would come by late at night and knock on his window.

One afternoon, as I was lying on my living room floor listening to the Beatles' album, "Sergeant Pepper's Lonely Hearts Club Band," I looked up and saw two guys wearing dark glasses standing over me. Both had handguns packed in their belts.

"Where's Doug?" they asked.

"He'll be here in a minute," I said, taking off my headphones.

"We'll just hang around. We're here to pick up a package," they said. With that, they dropped a thick stack of bills on the floor. It had to have been thousands of dollars. I unplugged the headphones, and we all listened to the music. After a few minutes, Doug showed up and completed the deal.

Before long, Doug began carrying a gun himself, a development that disturbed me.

"What've you got a gun for?" I asked him.

"In this business," he said, "you need one."

After one large buy, our living room was crowded with hundreds of pounds of marijuana arranged in waist-high piles. Doug had driven a camper down to Mexico and brought a truck load of dope back across the border. We invited some people over for a cleaning party, smoking a little while we worked. Doug's pistol was lying on the coffee table.

"How do you work this thing?" I asked him.

"Cock it back," he said. "It's not loaded."

I thought it would be fun to fool around and scare my roommates.

I started waving the gun around, putting on a little Matt Dillon act.

"Okay, it's time for you and me to have a little shootout," I said to a friend of mine who was visiting from New York.

The guys were laughing at the two city boys playing Wild, Wild West. I cocked the gun back and pressed the trigger.

"BBBBBOOOOOOOOMMMMMM!"

Everyone sprang to attention, eyes wide. Several people rushed into the kitchen where we were. My New York friend turned white. The gun had been pointed toward a fellow named Gus. The bullet passed right over his head and pierced the wall.

The room was completely still, like a frozen frame on a videotape. No one moved. No one said a word. I set the gun down on the table, turned around and walked out the door. I went to Holly's place and didn't come back for two days. In those forty-eight hours, I replayed that scene again and again, chilled by what had so nearly happened. My recklessness nearly cost someone his life.

I grew more and more uncomfortable in the apartment as the drug deals escalated in size and frequency. It seemed like it was time to make a move, so I found a place two blocks off the Berkeley campus above the Wing Lee Laundromat, overlooking Telegraph Avenue. The move took me to the nucleus of some of the most radical causes of the '60s. On Telegraph Avenue, the bizarre was commonplace: bodies, busses, and buildings painted in psychedelic colors; a hell-fire preacher on one corner; a satanist gathering a crowd across the street; bald-headed devotees of eastern religions asking passers-by for donations. Visit a restaurant, and a customer's dog might be wandering around under the tables, unnoticed.

On the corner adjacent to my apartment was a Hell's Angels hangout where bearded bikers wheeled up the pavement in their low-slung Harley-Davidsons. One apartment in my building housed several members of the Students for a Democratic Society. (The SDS was in the news for allegedly burning down buildings.) With the 1968 Democratic National Convention coming up soon in Chicago, I listened in periodically as they espoused their political views with great intensity.

My family had no idea of the lifestyle in which I was immersed.

When they announced their plans to visit, I dreaded thinking about how they would react to my new surroundings. Not only were my parents flying out to California, but they were bringing my younger brother and sister as well. I warned my roommates to be on their best behavior, but I was nervous. I would have to perform a juggling act to cover up my lifestyle and convince them that everything was okay with me.

"I want this place clean," I told my roommates the day before my family was to arrive. "My mother's going to be here tomorrow to check things out."

"No problem," they assured me. "It'll be clean."

Once the family arrived, I parked them at the Fairmount Hotel, a respectable place, and spent the night with them there.

"Why don't we take a look at your place?" my mother said the next day.

"Oh, why don't we take a little tour of San Francisco," I suggested, hoping the alternative would distract her. It didn't work. She wanted to see where her son was living.

I tried to prepare her. "Well, I've got a nice place here in Berkeley," I started off. "But you might notice it's a different kind of neighborhood. Some of the people might look a little, well, hippie-ish to you."

When we pulled up on Telegraph Avenue, my mother didn't even want to get out of the car. Here she was, a middle-aged, middle-class Republican from Long Island visiting the radical left fringe of the counterculture.

"Look at these people," she said incredulously, motioning toward half-naked men with bead necklaces and waist-long pony tails. My mother was never one to hide her feelings. She turned to my father and said, "Get him outta here!"

Finally she settled down a bit, and we all went upstairs to my apartment. When I swung open the front door, it was immediately clear that the plea to my roommates had been ignored. The place was a trash heap. Adorning the middle of the room was a big garbage barrel filled with chicken bones and beer cans from the previous night's party. To round out my family's first impression, somebody was standing in the middle of the living room, lifting weights, dressed in nothing but his cotton briefs. I had never seen him before.

My worst fears were coming to pass. "Get your clothes on and get lost," I told the stranger, as my mother hid my little sister behind her.

I parted the strings of beads that served as the doorway into my bedroom and gave her a tour of the rest of the apartment. She noticed that the stereo setup was the only furniture in the place. The pungent scent of incense hung in the air. I'm not sure whether she recognized that most of the greenery adorning the window sills was illegal. Regardless, she was horrified. She started crying.

My father appeared perfectly calm, but he, too, was stunned by what he saw. "Where did we go wrong?" my father asked, searching for a way to make sense of my lifestyle. It confused him to find me choosing what he saw as a degrading life when I could have had so much more.

He started talking about the sacrifices my grandparents had made to come to this country. "They wanted a better life for their children," he told me.

My grandfather, an Italian seaman, had jumped ship in Canada and had found a job building a rail line. He had swung a pick until his hands bled, slept in a rail car, and earned fifty cents a day. Once he got to New York City, he spent his working years as a night watchman working in the freezer of an ice cream plant, and laboring on an assembly line in a chemical factory.

My grandmother's entry to this country was more of a nightmare than a dream come true, my father reminded me. After joining the immigrants' celebration as they lifted their children up to get a glimpse of the Statue of Liberty, she stepped off the boat and was greeted with the news that her mother had died, leaving her to care for her brothers and sisters. Her dream of an education had vanished; instead she struggled to survive, spending her next thirty-five years dressing dolls in a sweat shop.

Considering the price my family had paid to carve out a good life in this country, my father couldn't understand why I was sleeping on the floor when I could afford a bed, why I was living above a laundromat when I could have been enjoying the beautiful Long Island house he had worked all his life to afford, a house I had begged him to buy only two years before. "What did we ever do that would make you want to live like this?" he asked, as if he wanted me to explain how I could so easily discard what others had sacrificed so much to provide. . . .

As I headed toward the terminal exit, I kept thinking about how the dream that had started off with such promise had spread such devastation. My parents were heartbroken because their son was throwing his life away.

Doug's plan to make a few fast bucks had made him into front page news in the *San Francisco Chronicle* and had won mention in *The New York Times.* Just a few months after I moved out, he was arrested for his role in a narcotics ring that involved a thousand employees at the automobile plant in Fremont. It didn't seem real, that instead of going to scuba diving school, my ex-roommate was probably going to prison.

John's heavy drug use continued to increase, and now Holly was heading as far east as she could go, the path of her life forever altered.

I looked around the airport terminal and noticed young children hugging arriving grandparents and waving to departing dads. One day, I realized, I would have a child as old as these. Amid all the sorrow I felt for Holly, my friends and my family, my heart ached most for one not even born yet, one who would grow up without knowing her father.

Finally, finding no way to fight the despair, I left the terminal and slid into my car. I turned the radio on and listened to the broadcaster announce in a quavering voice that Robert Kennedy, on a campaign swing through California, had been shot as he walked through the kitchen of a Los Angeles hotel. He was dead.

THE MISSING YEARS

Tears streamed from the eyes of the little girl sitting in my office. I had known her and her mother since they had become part of our church the year before. This child had crystal blue eyes, blushing cheeks, and all the life and carefree exuberance of any eight-year-old. My wife and I had stopped by their home to visit, and I'd watched her carry around her favorite stuffed animals, race her bicycle in the street, and join clusters of friends carrying on the non-stop chatter and giggles of that age. But today, the deep sobs of this child before me represented some very grownup emotions.

She had always lived without a father—had never seen his face, never known his name. She was by herself visiting her aunt in another city when the aunt told her that her father lived just a few houses down the street.

So with an unimaginable array of fears, emotions, and questions turning inside her, she gathered up her courage, walked up, and knocked on his door. As it turned out, the aunt had been mistaken. This man had known the girl's mother but was not the father.

"Not me, kid," he said. "I'm not your father."

The cold reception the little girl received crushed a vulnerable place deep in her heart. After the girl had returned from her trip, her mother called me. Now her daughter was in my office, overcome by disappointment, facing the reality that she might never find her father. She had wanted so badly to know him—whoever he was, wherever he lived—even if he weren't the greatest man around. She wanted his love, his approval. Somewhere, her father was out there. Didn't he want to see her? Didn't he care at all?

I was stricken inside. I wrapped her in my arms, and she buried her head in my chest. I rocked her as we wept together, her sorrow mingling with mine.

As we waded through this wave of emotion, my mind drifted to another little girl, a child who would be only a year or two older than the one I was holding. Had she also wept on someone else's shoulder as she searched for reasons to believe that her father loved her?

More than a decade had passed since that dreary airport farewell with Holly in California. After we had said good-bye, only one brief phone call from the East Coast had bridged the continent between our separate lives. She had called to say she'd had the baby, a girl, and that she had named her Heidi. Those were the closing words of the short chapter of life we had shared together, and neither of us expected it to be opened again.

I had not seen any reason to carve a place in Holly's new life since she had flown some three thousand miles to get away from me. Assuming she would marry, I couldn't picture myself intruding as a second father in a family in which I was an unpleasant reminder of something best forgotten. No, I wasn't going to try any heroics; I'd probably mess things up more than I already had. So with a mixture of resignation and relief, I had accepted the finality of it all. We hadn't exchanged addresses or phone numbers. We hadn't said "Keep in touch." It had just been, "Good-bye."

The many years that had come and gone had frayed the few thin threads that linked our lives. Now, the separation seemed irreversible. But the intervening years did nothing to ease the burden of knowing I had brought a little girl into the world but was doing nothing to help her.

As I wrapped my arms tightly around the sobbing child in my office, her tears brought back the ache deep inside where I had tucked away my thoughts and feelings about Heidi. How ironic, I thought, that this girl would look to me as her pastor, while another little girl didn't even know I was her father. So much had changed, I thought, since my days in California. . . .

Once a week some friends and I played cards in our California apartment—nothing serious, just a little nickel-ante poker. One weekend, they announced they had met some girls, and the new acquaintances were coming over to go swimming. We were in the middle of our regular card game when our visitors showed up. It turned out that these girls were from a church group.

As we talked, I particularly noticed one whose name was Dawn. Despite the unreceptive atmosphere among my card-playing buddies, she kept directing the conversation to the Bible. Having grown up Catholic, I wasn't accustomed to her kind of intensity. But I was intrigued, and she invited me to church.

The night I was to go, I went to dinner with her family beforehand. While they dressed in suits and skirts, I showed up wearing my customary cut-offs and wine-stained T-shirt.

That night was the first time I had ever been in a Protestant church. People raised their hands. I thought it was weird, but I didn't mind them doing what they wanted to do as long as they didn't try to make me be like them.

During the next several months, as my California life continued to unravel, I drove down the coast to Dawn's town periodically and went to church with her family. They seemed to welcome me in their home, and my time with them was a refreshing change of pace from the countercultural world of Berkeley.

One night, when I had again come with them to church, I sat in the pew staring into the distance. The preacher was talking in the front, but I was oblivious to what he was saying. I was thinking about where my life had been and where it was going. My helplessness seemed to have caught up with me.

My life had been like a speeding locomotive charging toward its destination. From within the train were coming alarming noises, muffled by the roar of the engine. The warning signs had disturbed me, but I hadn't wanted to slow down. Then it was as if suddenly someone had pulled the emergency switch.

Holly's pregnancy had made me stop short and examine my life and realize how much damage had been done. I could no longer fill my life with fun; heartache had stripped that away. As much as I had tried to avoid it, I was forced to look inside myself and think.

I hadn't realized the degree of selfishness that motivated me. I'm bad, I had thought, but I'm not as bad as some people. But this pregnancy had eliminated all my comparisons. There was no comfort in thinking someone else was worse—that maybe somebody out there had fathered several kids and didn't care about any of them. That didn't make me feel any better.

I was jolted into facing the truth that I had blown it. I had reaped the results of my self-serving mentality. How many people would have to suffer because of me? The consequences would ripple for generations.

I had heard about Jesus since I was a small boy, but I had always responded with arguments. How can we be sure God exists? How do we know which religion's right? How can we prove the Bible is true? But I was no longer interested in philosophical discussions or religious debates. Desperation had swallowed up all my questions. No intellectual sparring match, regardless of the outcome, could resolve my heartache. I needed to draw on a power greater than myself because my mistakes were bigger and stronger than I was. I couldn't undo what I had done. I knew that night I deserved the ultimate penalty for the way I was, for the things I had done, for the suffering I had caused.

I needed to say I was sorry to someone. Not to people who would just pat me on the shoulder and say, "That's okay. We all have problems." But to someone who could understand how deeply sorry I was and how desperately I wanted life to be different. I could probably clean up my act—stop doing drugs, change some of my bad habits—but I couldn't remove the selfishness.

After the church service was over, people were milling around in the back. But I couldn't ignore this feeling of urgency to apologize for the way I was. And I felt like I had to know whether there was a God to hear me.

I got up from where I was seated and made my way to the front of the church, where I found a vacant corner. I knelt down. My words lacked eloquence, but they came from deep inside.

"I'm sorry," I said. "I'm sorry I was born. I'm sorry I've caused the problems I've caused. I'm sorry for the world I live in. It's so confusing, so full of selfishness. I don't know what I believe. I would like to know, Jesus, if you are really alive, if you are really God, if all these things that I have heard about you are true . . . . "

In the midst of these thoughts, I felt pressure on my shoulder, like a hand. Someone had come to console me, I assumed, but when I opened my eyes and turned around, no one was there.

Immediately, as I knelt in an isolated corner of that church building, I felt as if I were surrounded by the presence of the God I had been addressing. I had a clear sense of a choice presented to me. I could say to this unseen person who was near, "Yes, stay with me." Or I could say, "Please leave me alone."

I made my choice: I wanted him. Just then, it seemed as if that hand penetrated my body and swept right through me. I began to cry, sobbing deeply. I knew then that Jesus was real, and that nothing else mattered except knowing him. I knew that what the Bible said was true. And I knew that I was changed. "Jesus is real," I said, over and over, utterly amazed.

As I lingered at the front of the sanctuary, I asked him to do just one thing for someone I cared about: "There is a child I won't know and who won't know me," I told him. "Please take care of her."

I pressed the little girl in my office close to me. I couldn't erase her pain, but at least I could hold her, comfort her, and show her a glimpse of a father's affection. It wasn't much compared to what she needed, but it was all I could offer. And it was more than I could offer the child of mine whom I had never held.

As it did so often, a cloud of sadness and regret settled over me. Despite the years that had passed, I still had to face the sense of anguish that would return from time to time, the queasiness in my stomach that I had come to recognize as guilt. Some days, the past gnawed at my mind for hours. It was like an itch beneath a cast, begging for relief; yet nothing I could do would make any difference.

At times the weight of my thoughts of Heidi would be enough to nearly crush my hopes and convince me that I had no business doing what I was doing—pastoring a church. How could a person like me, a person who had lived as I had lived, speak on God's behalf? Never mind that I had been to Bible college. Never mind that I stood up in the front of a church every week and talked to people about the Bible. I knew I was just as needy as any one listening to me.

Only one antidote could ease my anguish. I had to reach back into the reservoir of truth that had been deposited in me as I knelt in the front of that California church: Jesus had forgiven me. I had to remind myself of that whenever my guilt returned to taunt me. Even though it didn't seem fair, though it didn't seem like I deserved mercy, God had made it clear on many occasions that he did not hold my mistakes against me.

I remembered one particular night while I was in Bible college and was visiting a church to hear my friends sing. I was struck once again with the truth that God's kindness was greater than my failure. . . .

A clear, melodious voice rose across the auditorium. The voice belonged to my friend, Naomi, who was singing a song adapted from Jesus Christ Superstar. As the sound carried to my seat during this service, the lyrics somehow found their way into a remote corner of my soul:

> *I don't know why he loves me.*
> *Why he came to save me*
> *I just don't know.*

As she was singing, I was overwhelmed by how kind God had been to me. I deserved only punishment for the wreckage I had made of my life and especially for the child out there who would grow up without knowing her father. God had found me in such a mess that night in California, yet he was gentle with me and so willing to look past my wrongs. I felt like there was nothing in me I could offer God in return. It was so bewildering.

I don't know why he loves me.
Why he came to save me
I just don't know. . . .

I crumpled to the floor, weeping, thinking about Heidi. Was she alone? Afraid? I wanted to be able to touch her, to hold her in my arms; I wanted to tell her I was sorry. I wanted to do something to make up for my failure.

But that night, I understood in a profound way that nothing I could ever do—no amount of personal sacrifice, good deeds, or religious perfection—would make up for the hurt I had caused Heidi. Nor could I undo any of the other things I had done wrong. But somehow Jesus showed me in a deeper way that he didn't hold my past against me. He accepted me in my imperfection. There was nothing more for me to do but to love him.

In my office, the little girl's sobs had softened now, and she gently pulled away from my shoulder. Though my embrace hadn't erased her sorrow, I could tell that it helped her to have someone to hold onto. I pulled a tissue off my desk and offered it to her. With a slight tremble still in her lips, she looked at me and smiled. "Thank you," she said.

As she stepped out of my office door, I sat quietly and began thinking about others in the church I had talked with about the blows of life that they had endured. Though not every counseling session was as intense as this one, as pastor of this church in Columbia, Missouri, I had spent much of my time over the last several years helping people face their confusion, pain, and guilt. Many, trying to come to terms with long-buried hurts, talked to me about the invisible wounds they bore, often from circumstances they could do nothing to change.

Some of the people in my office had wondered aloud, as they faced their despair, how I could relate to their situation. "You've got everything going for you," they would say, knowing nothing of the burden I carried. "You're successful. You've got a wife. Children.

Friends. People respect you. You could never understand how hard life is. You could never feel the way I do." Yet I did understand their hidden hurts to a degree many of them could not comprehend.

One afternoon I was called to the University of Missouri Hospital emergency room to see the parents of a five-year-old boy whose mother would occasionally visit our church. As he was getting off his bus after kindergarten that morning, the boy dropped some papers and reached down to pick them up. The bus driver pulled away without noticing the boy had slipped into the path of the wheels. When I arrived, the doctor had just told these parents their little boy was dead. It was one of the most heart-breaking scenes I had ever witnessed.

People facing this kind of pain could not be comforted by simple religious cliches. The raw places in their lives needed a healing that I could not produce. Though I couldn't answer the many questions they had or the "why's" that plagued them, I did feel I could offer them the one commodity that had carried me this far. I could offer them hope—hope that Jesus is a real person who understands the pain of life.

I could tell them about a person who had grieved over a lost loved one, someone who had felt the ache of repeated rejection and the betrayal that came by the kiss of a friend. Jesus knew what it was to be misunderstood, maligned, and abused. He knew what it was like to suffer alone. This man, though he came from heaven, did not go through life unscathed. He was spared no agony. He made himself vulnerable, and it killed him.

The God I had to offer people is affected when we cry to him in pain. He doesn't listen to our pleas with the unfeeling logic of a supercomputer sorting through a calculation. He feels our wounds. He bears our suffering and takes our sorrow upon himself. He cares deeply about our hurts. This was the only reality I found substantial enough to help people walk through their emotional combat zones. This hope was all I had found to cling to in my private despair. It was the only real antidote I had known to the pain of life.

All these thoughts emerged as I sat quietly at my desk. I was still recovering from the emotional encounter with the girl who had just left my office, as well as from the other feelings her turmoil had stirred. I needed to turn my attention to other matters, other appointments, other items on my "To Do" list, but it was hard to change gears. I would take just a few more minutes, I decided, to clear my mind.

It seemed strange to me that I had ended up in the position I was. I could never think of myself as religious, never could see myself as a "preacher." I knew myself too well. At times, I struggled wondering if I were in the right "business." I wasn't one who had answers for everyone. I wasn't one who could hold up my performance record and prove my ability to represent God.

So to the group that had banded together to form this church, I had never offered any impeccable credentials showing my qualifications for leadership. "I'm not a theologian," I told them. "I'm not a great preacher or a real disciplined, holy guy. But I know Jesus has forgiven me."

My satisfaction came from getting to know God and from relating closely with the people I was linked with in the church. But I could never escape the enduring sorrow from the one relationship that had never even had a chance to begin.

I got up from my desk and walked slowly toward the door. I wondered if Heidi, like the little girl who had left my office a few minutes before, was hurting from not knowing her real father. Was anyone helping her face her pain? Or had someone stepped into her life to fill the gap left by my absence? I didn't know, and the answers were beyond my reach.

"Please take care of her," I prayed once again silently, as I had so many times over the years. "Please take care of Heidi."

5

THE DOORBELL

Traffic going out to Long Island was heavy. I was approaching the exit where I was planning a brief stop. My mother had purchased a sportcoat for me; it had been altered and would be waiting for me at a clothing store near the next off ramp.

Suddenly, something snapped under the hood. The steering wheel began tightening up, and I knew immediately that the power steering was going out. Terrific! I thought. My mother's car. That's all I need. What am I doing here anyway?

Once again, my mind replayed the debate of whether I should be making this New York trip in the first place. I had so many responsibilities to take care of back home in Missouri; a week away from the office was putting me that much further behind. But a close friend had urged me to come. He was speaking here at a church leaders conference. He was a stranger in New York. Since I knew the city and the conference hosts, he had asked me to come along to help him get acquainted and to lend moral support.

But I had already traveled as much as I wanted to in 1986, having taken two trips overseas and spoken several places in the United States. The increasing invitations to step out of my regular duties at the church and travel to other places added to an already burdened schedule. Since I wasn't slated to speak, it didn't seem essential; I wondered how worthwhile it would be to invest an entire week of my time here.

The proposed trip to New York had come during a pivotal time at home. We were preparing for a leaders conference of our own; some two hundred people would be descending on our church in a month. Not only did we need to finalize the speaking schedule and topics, but we needed to be sure all the arrangements were complete to provide housing and meals for this crowd for nearly a week.

Responding to my friend's request would mean that things at the office would be all the more crazy when I returned. If this trip weren't absolutely necessary, it didn't seem worth the trouble. My wife and secretary had both encouraged me to go; the ticket had already been purchased. But the day I was to leave, I was still deliberating whether to call and back out.

When the last minute had arrived and I had to make a decision, I had rested my head in my hands. "Lord, what do you want me to do?" I had asked, hoping the prayer would clear the confusion. It didn't seem to.

"I'm going," I had told my secretary, glancing at my watch. Departure time was less than an hour away. I drove home, threw some clothes into a bag, said good-bye, and rushed out the door— still not sure why I was making the trip.

Now I was wondering all the more why I had come to New York, since I had to deal with this car trouble. Maybe I should try to find a service station, I thought to myself as I continued down that congested New York expressway. No, that won't work, I concluded. It's a foreign car. Most stations wouldn't be able to handle it.

I'll just drive on to the house, I thought, charging past the exit I had planned to take. The engine might get a little hot, but I think it'll make it.

I had been staying with my parents on Long Island, driving into the city each morning for the conference, then returning late at night after the meetings concluded. This was Tuesday afternoon, and after the morning session I had decided to return to Long Island even though it would be a full hour's drive there and another hour back before the evening session began. It had started to rain that morning, and I'd had second thoughts. But this would be the only time my father would be home during the day that week, and I was eager to see him, so I had headed out, despite the rain, the long drive, and the full conference agenda.

I probably should have just stayed at the conference, I thought, fighting the steering wheel. But at last, I made it home. When I pulled in the driveway, the engine was hissing and steam was surging from the hood.

Inside, I gave my dad the bad news about the car and started looking through the phone book for a mechanic. My father was reading the newspaper on the couch; my mother was in the kitchen, preparing dinner.

The doorbell rang. "Could you get that, Joseph?" my mother asked.

"I'm on the phone," I said. "Besides, who's going to want me? I haven't lived here for twenty years."

"Oh, get the door," she insisted.

A STRANGER'S STORY

"May I speak to Joe Tosini?" asked a casually dressed, middle-aged man at the door.

"I'll get him," I replied, assuming he was looking for my father.

"I believe I'm looking for you," the man said. He mentioned a name: Hollis. It was a formal name . . . it didn't register. I offered him a blank stare. He went on.

"You are aware that you have a seventeen-year-old daughter, aren't you?" he asked. My entire world crashed to a stop.

I stepped outside, pulling the door shut behind me. We walked down the driveway, and the man offered his story. He was Hollis'— Holly's—husband, he explained. They lived together in Maryland, where he worked in the construction business. He was in New York waiting for some materials to arrive for a job. He had called to tell Holly he was delayed, adding that he was planning to take a drive out to Long Island.

She suggested that if he had time, he might stop by to see if the parents of Heidi's father still lived in the same place. She had dug up this eighteen-year-old address. Perhaps they would know of his whereabouts, she told him. Heidi was preparing to graduate from high school, and Holly thought she might be ready to meet her father. His story stunned me; my mind was racing with anticipation.

"Look, I just got here five minutes ago," I said. "I don't even live in New York, I live in Missouri. In fact, I haven't lived here for twenty years. I was just here for a conference and decided to drive out to my parents' home for the afternoon."

"Isn't that interesting," he said, apparently intrigued by the circumstances.

"Besides that," I added, "I wouldn't have even been here to answer the door except for the fact that I had to skip a stop on the way home because the car was acting up." We were both struck by the string of circumstances that had brought the two of us together at the same place and time.

"This must be fate," he said. I didn't argue.

My father opened the front door and stepped outside, looking concerned. "Is everything all right?" he asked, curious as to why I hadn't invited the man in.

"Yeah, fine," I said, nonchalantly. "We're just having a conversation out here. I'll be inside in a little bit."

He was still puzzled, but he turned and went back into the house. "What do you do in Missouri?" the man asked.

"I'm a pastor." Now it was his turn to look shocked.

"Uh. . . I wasn't under the impression that you were a minister," he said, seeming a bit puzzled. "As a matter of fact, I had the idea that either you'd be flying drugs across the border of Mexico or you'd be in the Mafia."

In the next few minutes, I told him my part of the story, beginning with California and our airport farewell on that June day in 1968 when Robert Kennedy was assassinated. The only time I had talked to Holly since, I told him, was during a quick phone call when she had told me the baby had been born.

"I really didn't know Holly that long . . ." I said, not knowing how much information to give him. He interrupted me, as if to say he didn't require any more details.

"Look, Heidi is the only child she has," he said, "and I don't know if she wants you to meet her or not." Obviously, Holly had no idea what kind of man she might find after almost twenty years. She was apparently making sure that if her worst imaginations had come true, she and her daughter could remain safely out of reach.

My mind was whirring with a hundred questions. Yet with so much at stake, I dared not push. I just tried to keep the conversation going, absorbing every sentence.

He said the two of them had been married eight years but had no children. Holly had been single during most of Heidi's growing up years.

"Heidi's a pleasant girl," he said. "She doesn't give me any problems." I thought it seemed strange he would speak of her in such detached terms.

"I have children of my own," he added. He didn't aspire to be a father to Heidi, and he didn't pretend to have parental rights.

"She's Holly's child, not mine," he said, making it clear that Holly would be the decision maker in this situation.

This family portrait was much different from what I had envisioned; it had one parent, not two. All the assumptions I'd pieced together eighteen years ago were being dismantled in an instant. Heidi didn't grow up thinking some other man was her father; she grew up without a father! As the reality broke over me, I groped to reconstruct my private world with the revelation that Heidi needed a father.

I can't let this guy go, I thought. He was my link to the child I had never known. He could walk away, never to be heard from again. But I have to keep cool, I thought, and not scare him by coming on too strongly.

"Do you have any pictures?" I asked, trying to hide my desperation. He didn't.

"Well, what does Heidi look like?" I asked.

"She's a lovely girl, about five-foot-eight," he said, studying my features. "Yeah, I can see a resemblance."

"Can you tell me where you live?" I asked, probing for as much information as I could get.

"No, I can't do that," he said. "Holly doesn't want you to know where she is. I'm just here checking out the situation; I'll let her know what I'm finding out. If she wants to get in contact with you, she will."

That comment set off panic inside. What if she decided not to reach me? I couldn't let him get away.

"Can you give me your name?" I asked, thinking at least I would have something to go on. I pulled out a piece of paper and scribbled it down. I gave him my address and phone number in Missouri.

"Please call me," I said, almost pleading.

"I don't know, but I think Holly will probably contact you," he said, sizing up our conversation. "But that's up to her; she has a mind of her own."

We shook hands, and he walked back toward the street, climbed into his pickup, and drove off. I stood there for a few minutes, shell-shocked, trying to organize my thoughts. For eighteen years, Heidi and I had lived in separate realms. Now, during the course of a fifteen-minute conversation, our worlds had touched.

For the first time, I realized my entrance into Heidi's life wouldn't be an intrusion on another man's territory. Better to let her continue believing someone else was her father, I had concluded years before, than to break up an otherwise happy home by demanding my due as a biological parent. But no nurturing father figure had ever filled the void of my absence. Until now, I had known only my own pain. But standing on that driveway, I began to feel a link with the grief of a young girl facing the storms of life without a father to brace her.

She needs me, I thought. She needs someone to help guide her, support her, love her. With my feelings of fatherhood awakened, finding her took on a sense of urgency. I had to let her know I cared, that I had cared these many years. But how? With only a name and a state? This man had planted a seed of hope that the time had come to meet her. But would it really happen? Would she even want to know me?

Suddenly, another burst of panic shot through me. I had to get back inside the house. The longer I stayed outside, the more reason my parents would have to suspect something out of the ordinary. This wasn't the time to tell them. But how could I just stroll back in, as if nothing had happened? I went into the house, my heart pounding. Dinner was ready; they were waiting for me. "Who was that?" my father asked, as I sat down at the table.

"It was somebody who knew an old friend of mine from California," I said carefully, keeping my voice void of any fluctuation. "My friend wanted to know where I was these days, so this guy looked up your address while he was in New York."

"What did he want?" my father said, prying a little further.

"Just wanted to know where I was. So I gave him my address in Missouri," I said. "He's going to give it to my friend, and then they'll probably contact me there." I looked down at my plate, pushing my portion from one side to the other. Silence. That seemed to satisfy them.

When I got back to the conference that night, I was in a daze. A good friend of mine noticed I was distracted and asked me what was wrong. I welcomed the chance to sort out the events of the day, so we went back to his room and I told him the story.

As it turned out, he had a story of his own. He hadn't seen his dad until his teens. He eased some of my tension with assurances that Heidi would be thrilled to find out I was her father.

I had walked through the rest of the New York conference in a stupor, completely preoccupied. I'd given my wife, Dawn, a hint that I had some big news for her. "This has been the most significant day of my life," I had said on the telephone, but I wanted to wait to tell her about it in person.

"You'd better sit down for this one," I told Dawn when I got home from New York. "This has been quite a week."

We walked upstairs together. I set my bag down on the bed. Dawn sat on the floor.

"Did we find our big sister?" she said, having had a day to think about what my dramatic news could be. Dawn had always referred to Heidi as part of our family, as an older sister to our other two daughters, Jodi and Joy.

"How did you know?" I asked.

"It just seemed the way you were talking on the phone. . ." she said, "I thought this was probably it. I knew eventually we would make contact."

I told her the story of Holly's husband ringing the doorbell and the flood of feelings our encounter released. And I told her he wouldn't tell me where they lived or offer me any assurance that we would get together.

Dawn was optimistic. She told me not to panic, saying things would happen in God's timing.

I was excited to tell the news to the church's leadership team, nine men who shared the pastoral duties. These men were my friends. I had told them about my California days, and most of them knew about Heidi and the heartache she represented. There was little pretense in this group. We were not professionals who happened to be working there because of the career rewards; we had come together for a reason we thought was more significant. We believed that God had joined our lives and families together in the cause of establishing a strong church. They were very supportive as I recounted the story of my encounter at my parents' front door.

"Obviously, God is in this," one assured me.

I shared how desperate I was to find Heidi right away. "She'll want to contact you," another said confidently.

"How do you think the church will handle this?" I asked. We talked about the best way to share the story with the congregation. The men agreed that the congregation would be supportive.

"I wonder if there will be a few who will be upset, though," one said.

"Why? He wasn't even a Christian then," another responded.

"That doesn't matter," was the reply. "There could still be some people, especially the older ones, who would be pretty uncomfortable at the thought of their pastor fathering an illegitimate child."

"Not in this church," the other replied.

The prospect of sharing my story with the church was not alarming to me. Every group has its own personality, with certain strengths and weaknesses. Our church had been launched by a group of mostly college-age converts, and we had a combination of enthusiasm and ignorance, idealism and inexperience. Our imperfections were apparent. But this church's personality was such that when someone's failure was exposed, there was room to be embarrassed. When people would openly share their weaknesses, whether in a small home fellowship group or in a more public meeting, I had seen more of a desire to comfort and forgive than to judge and expel. I was certain the compassion I had seen offered to others would be extended to me as well.

Heidi was such an obsession those days I could barely conduct a conversation. My mind would drift to thoughts of her, wondering what she was like, what she thought about, how she talked, how much she might look like me. As my thoughts wandered toward that place in my heart where Heidi had been hidden all these years, often my throat would tighten up and tears would come. Day and night, I tried to imagine that first encounter. What would it be like?

The church secretaries were getting irritated with me. Between my office and their work area, I repeatedly would pace back and forth. "I'm expecting a phone call from the East Coast," I said. "Be sure to put it through immediately." I must have repeated some variation of those instructions more than a dozen times over those next few days, just to make sure nothing broke down on my end.

The uncertainty of whether or not they would make contact seemed to be more than I could bear. I agonized through those days, waiting . . . waiting . . . waiting . . . .

My friends were encouraging me to be patient, not to force matters. "Relax, Joe," someone told me. "Maybe they need time to think things over. It might be six months before they call."

Six months! I thought. *No way.* Finally, I just couldn't take it anymore. I decided to try a little investigative work. I got out a map and jotted down some cities and towns in Maryland. Then I started calling directory assistance, checking the listings. After a dozen or so attempts, I found the name that matched the one the man had given me at my parents' house. The listing was for a small community outside of Washington, D.C. The operator gave me the number.

Now what? I forced myself to relax and think the matter through. Don't blow it, I thought. Holly said she would decide whether to get in touch. But I can't stand to just sit here and do nothing. What could it hurt just to give her a call?

Where would Heidi be? It wouldn't be good if she answered. I needed to talk to Holly first—definitely. But it was morning, only an hour later on the coast. So Heidi would be in school. I thought I'd give it a try.

I dialed the number. . . .

"Brrrrnnnnggg." I got through.

"Brrrrnnnnggg." I heard a click. My throat tightened. I sat forward, ready to bridge an eighteen-year chasm.

"You have reached the home of . . . ."

A recording. But it was the voice of the man I had talked with in New York. It was the right number. A surge of relief went through me. I was getting close.

I waited once more. Leaning back in my chair, I rehearsed what I would say over and over, imagining what Holly would say . . . after all these years.

I tried calling the next day. Again, the recording answered. I would have to wait again.

Finally, on the third day, I picked up the phone once again and punched in the number.

"Brrrrnnnnggg."

"Hello." It wasn't the answering machine. It was Holly's voice.

"Hello, Holly?"

"Yes."

"This is Joe. . . ."

7

*H*ELLO AGAIN

"I have something very serious to talk to you about," I told Jodi and Joy, instructing them to come into my bedroom. Dawn had agreed that it would be better to wait to talk to our twelve- and thirteen-year-old girls until we had a little more information to give them. Now was the time.

They sat down and soberly awaited my announcement. "Do you remember hearing me tell people about my life before I became a Christian?" They nodded. "I really did a lot of wrong things," I said, "some hurtful things."

This was turning out to be even more difficult than I had thought. All their lives they had known me as their father, who happened to be a pastor. I didn't know what effect the news I was about to break to them would have. It wouldn't be easy for them.

"When I lived in California, before I married Mom, I had a relationship with a woman. . ." I explained, slowing my pace to make sure they understood every word. . . "who got pregnant and had a baby girl." Now they sat up straight, leaning closer to me, their eyes wide. "I never saw the baby," I said. "In fact, I never saw the woman again after she left California."

I told them of the recent chain of events that had led to my phone call with Holly. "I'm leaving tomorrow to go to Maryland," I said. "Her name is Heidi, and there's a chance I might get to see her."

Holly had agreed on the phone for me to fly out there and talk things over with her. She would tell Heidi I was there, she said, and let her decide whether she wanted to see me. The girls looked away, pensively.

"I'm very sorry I have to tell you this, but we've been praying for a long time that this day would come," I said. "So we're really excited and looking forward to what's going to happen." I paused to see how they were reacting. They were quiet. "I want you girls to know I love you," I said, slowly. "And I'm praying that this will be an exciting time for you, too." The tears started to fall. Both girls choked back gentle sobs. I encouraged them to take some time in their rooms to pray about this significant event about to take place. Then we would talk again, I said. About an hour later they returned.

"Here, Dad," Jodi said, handing me a folded piece of paper. Joy handed me one, too. "We want you to take these letters to Heidi tomorrow."

I hadn't known how the girls would handle the news. How do twelve- and thirteen-year-old minds think, I wondered. I read the notes and then handed them to Dawn. They answered all my questions. Shaking my head back and forth, I looked at the girls, floored by their response. God had caused something to grow inside these girls over their short lifespans. Silently, I thanked God for the sensitivity they were emanating.

"What does she look like, Dad?" they asked. "Does she know you're coming? Does she know about us?" Relaxed for the moment, knowing they had begun to open their hearts to their new sister, we talked through each question, letting our excitement show.

"Hey," Jodi said, a fresh realization striking her. "I'm not the oldest anymore."

Now, thirty-eight years old, I was getting off an airplane, saying hello to the woman who had left California in an airplane nearly two decades before. The reason for our meeting in 1986 was the same as our reason for parting in 1968: a girl named Heidi. We would talk together first, we had agreed, then figure out whether the time was right for me to meet Heidi. No promises from her; no pressure from me—those were the terms of the agreement.

As the plane taxied toward the gate, I got more fidgety than ever. My stomach was churning from hope laced with fear. What would happen today? I wondered. Would it turn out to be a huge disappointment? Was I just being set up? Was Holly bitter to the point that she would want to withhold Heidi from me? No point in expecting the worst, I thought.

Waiting for the passengers ahead to clamor off the plane, I clutched my bag and prepared for this face-to-face encounter with my past. "Thank you, Lord, so much for your mercy," I said quietly, waiting my turn to step into the aisle. "God, I need your wisdom." As the line of passengers diffused into the terminal, I stopped. I didn't see anyone I recognized. To the right, no one. To the left, no one. Suddenly I heard my name.

"Joe?" I saw her face.

"Hi, Holly. Good to see you again." I gave her a hug. As we began walking away from the gate, tears began welling up in her eyes. She excused herself and scurried off to the bathroom.

We massaged the initial tension with stray conversation: the congestion at the D.C. airport, the length of the drive, the conditions on the flight. We found her car, climbed in, and headed for the highway. It was Holly who took the first step beyond the chit chat.

"I talked to Heidi this morning," she said. "I told her to really consider seeing you today." Today, I thought. I hadn't even dreamed it could happen so soon. I smiled, carefully tempering my eagerness.

We stopped at a deli in their town and picked up something to eat. Then we headed for a park where we sat down at a picnic table for lunch. I remembered back to our last encounter in a park, three thousand miles to the west, where I had first found out about a coming child.

"Finish your sandwich," Holly said. "Because this is going to tear you up." Holly had brought a box full of pictures. At that picnic table, she introduced me to my child for the first time—in pictures. Photographs of her as a baby, as a young girl, and as a mature young woman.

Until then, I had only been able to conjure up images in my mind of a young girl whose name was Heidi. Now, for the first time, I could see her brown eyes, her freckled face, her auburn hair, her smile. The pictures now replaced the mental images that had inhabited my daydreams these years. It was more overwhelming than I had expected. With each picture I had to fight back fresh tears.

Holly was gentle with me, giving me time to react to each photo. Her demeanor was not vindictive. She had laid her past aside long ago; she was now allowing me to experience the bittersweet pleasure of becoming acquainted with this wonderful girl she had raised.

I had not known how she would regard me. But she was clearly respecting me as a co-parent, even though she had invested nearly two decades of her life rearing her alone.

We sat together on the bench for over an hour, letting the pictures chart the course through the missing years. There was Heidi wrapped in a baby blanket. Here she was blowing candles out on her second birthday. There she was decked out in a Brownie Scout uniform.

Holly supplemented the stories the photos depicted by telling me of the jobs she'd had, the places they'd lived, the struggles she'd faced as a single parent, and the joy of her only daughter.

Since our good-bye, my life had taken quite a turn, too, I told Holly, beginning to fill her in on my interim years. She was surprised I was living in Missouri rather than New York or California. I told her I had gotten married before leaving California, and that we had two daughters with another child on the way. But the piece of information that had shocked her the most was that I was now a pastor. It just didn't seem to fit, she thought.

I was eager to share with her the reasons for my change of direction, which had come shortly after she had flown to the East Coast. I wanted her to know how Heidi and she had helped me realize my emptiness, the corruption that was in me and that I could do nothing about.

"You know, Holly, I'm still me," I said. "But in many ways I'm a different guy. It's not just because I'm older. I've really had an alteration in my thinking and in my values. I've come to realize there is a God in heaven who is involved with our lives. He's not silent. He doesn't turn his head from us. Even though you've been raising Heidi alone all these years, he has not forsaken you. And I know," I added, "that it's in his timing that we're here today, seeing each other again."

She listened respectfully, yet some of what I was saying seemed foreign to her. She did recognize, though, that our meeting seemed to bear the mark of fate. Even the way her husband had spoken of his encounter with me in New York, she said, was remarkable. He thought it strange that such an uncanny string of coincidences had made that meeting possible and gotten this entire process started.

It was quiet for a few moments. I wanted to tell her so much more; but there would be more time. I picked up another picture.

"I brought Heidi to this park many times when she was younger," Holly said, smiling at the memories. "We used to come here to feed the ducks."

"This town is where she grew up," she said, adding that Heidi's school and their first home were close by.

I was delighted that Holly seemed eager to invite me into her past; she seemed glad to have found someone who shared such an interest in Heidi, the child who had been so important to her over the years. I wanted to know everything, I told her.

Leaving the box of pictures on the bench, we stood up and began strolling through the park. Holly took me back to the day she got off the plane in Maryland; she, too, remembered it as the day Robert Kennedy was shot.

She told me about a baby-sitter who had been like a second mother to Heidi, about her Catholic grade school, her interest and skill in art, her love for softball and tennis.

When we were ready to leave, my heart was full. Each fresh brush stroke of information—about Heidi's past, her personality, her interests, skills, and ambitions—painted a fuller portrait of this daughter I was just now getting to know.

When we got back to the motel, Holly planned to call Heidi to let her know that she would be home soon. But before she made the call, I told her I had something for her in my briefcase.

I pulled out the notes that Dawn, Jodi, and Joy had sent along. Holly opened them and began to read, starting with my wife's note to her:

Dear Holly,

I am sending this note along with Joe to make sure that my heart is expressed also.

The joy and relief and now the anticipation that we are feeling is difficult to put into words.

There have been so many emotions these past two weeks, as we have smiled and cried and cried and been uncontrollably preoccupied with this wonderful reality actually becoming a tangible part of our lives. We feel like God has chosen this time to give us a gift far greater than any we have ever prayed for.

We are filled with gratitude and respect for you, Holly. We know the difficulties (we counsel lots of single parents!) and sacrifices this has required of you.

I want to say personally that you and your family are so welcome in our home! You probably don't realize how blessed and delighted we would all be to have you here with us.

> *Love,*
> *Dawn*

Holly sat down on the bed, looking more surprised than anything. Our talk together that afternoon had convinced her that I was sincere in my desire to receive Heidi into my life; Dawn's letter began to convince her that the open reception included not only Heidi but her as well, and that it came not only from me but also from Dawn.

Without a word, she slowly folded the paper and opened the note Dawn had written Heidi:

Dear, dear Heidi,

It seems like a dream to be able to write this to you after almost eighteen years of having to suppress our desire to know you and be with you and to have you in your rightful place in our lives!

Things can never be the same for us, after the events of

the last two weeks. Finally knowing where you are and allowing our natural love and desires for you to be openly acknowledged has laid bare a part of our hearts that we have silently suppressed since you were born.

We longed for this day, Heidi, and are experiencing the gamut of fears of rejection and emotions I'm sure you are familiar with also.

Because we believe God is arranging this, we are confident it will all work out according to his plan.

This isn't a "one-time meeting" kind of thing Heidi. We want you in our lives and family for the rest of our lives.

I love you,
Dawn

She methodically folded Dawn's letter and slid it back into the packet. In silence, she pulled out the next note, this one from Jodi:

Dear Heidi,
Hi, I really am anxious to meet you.
My name is Jodi, I am 13. I just turned 13 August 6. We really hope that you will come and stay with us at our house sometime. Please send me a picture of you.

Also if you can, write me a letter.

I think my mom sent some pictures of me and some other people with my dad.

I am the one with the blond hair and a few freckles.

I am glad we are going to finally get to meet you. I hope you know that you're really wanted and loved here.

Love,
Jodi Tosini

Finally, she opened the last note, the one from Joy, my twelve-year-old:

Dear Heidi,

My name is Rachel Joy but everyone calls me Joy. I'm very excited to meet you. I only hope you want to meet me too.

As soon as my dad told me about you, I think God put a very special love in my heart for you. My mom is going to have a new baby in March. I told her that this new baby (your brother or sister) would have the privilege of knowing you all his life. I wish we could have grown up knowing each other. (By the way I just turned 12 September 2nd.)

My dad is going to tell our whole church about you, and I'm sure when he does, they're going to be thrilled to meet you, especially my friends.

From what my dad has told me about you, it sounds like we may look alike. I know you're busy with school, but if you get a chance, please write.

> *Love,*
> *your baby sister,*
> *R. Joy Tosini*

Sitting on the bed, Holly slumped over holding the letters in her lap, sobbing. It seemed as if the letters had somehow pried open a hidden part of her heart not often exposed. For several minutes I left her alone, allowing her to walk through her wave of pain and relief. As the sobs softened, I assured her that everything was going to be fine.

She took a few moments to gather herself and called Heidi.

"I'll be home in about fifteen minutes," Holly said over the phone. "We had a nice day. We went to the park."

She nodded at the response on the other end. "I have some very nice letters you'll have to read," she said, having halted the tears but not knowing how to communicate what she had just experienced. Again, she was quiet, listening to Heidi. "Okay, I'll talk to you when I get home." She put the phone down and turned to me. "I think Heidi will come," she said. "I'll call you in a little bit. You keep the pictures."

8

THE WAIT

Holly left me with the boxful of pictures and went to talk to Heidi about seeing me. If all went well, Holly said, she would be back in a couple of hours—with Heidi. The arrangement was that I would wait in my room. When they arrived in the lobby, Holly would call, and I would then go to the lobby to meet them.

So there was nothing to do but wait.

I should take a nap, I thought, so I stretched out on the bed, bending my arm over my eyes. The phone would wake me. It would be okay. Just relax, I instructed myself. Try to get some sleep.

As I lay in the motel room, my thoughts wandering the corridors of the past, I recalled the countless times I had asked God to take care of Heidi. "Thank you for your faithfulness," I prayed silently. Not a week had passed in the last eighteen years when I hadn't thought about that child. Now I was only moments away from seeing her in the lobby of this Maryland hotel.

I haven't slept in two nights, I thought. I need some rest. Turning over onto my side, I settled into the pillow and tried to slow my thoughts. But my mind began replaying a terrifying scene my imagination had created years before . . . .

"Hey, do you know who I am?"

I was at some national conference on the East Coast where I had just finished a rousing sermon about God wanting us to be faithful friends, parents, and leaders in the church when this girl appeared three feet in front of me, snarling.

"No, you don't know who I am, do you? Of course you don't. . . ." Her voice got louder and louder, the disdain increasing with the volume.

"Of course you don't, because you were never there when I needed you!" Now she was shouting. "You deserted me! You left me! You didn't even care enough to come find me! And now you're parading around like some self-righteous preacher!"

"You're a joke!" she screamed. My face burned red, humiliated in front of a crowd of people shocked by the outburst and waiting for me to issue my denial. But I had no denial to offer. Their disapproving glares were fully deserved.

She darted off through the crowd. . . .

Tossing on the bed, I shuddered slightly and opened my eyes. My hands had started sweating, my muscles were tense. It was the same reaction I always had when my imagination tortured me with that haunting drama, as it had so many times before.

I took a deep breath. Soon, I could sit face to face with the child I feared meeting in some surprise confrontation. This reunion, I hoped, would forever end my most dreaded nightmare. But I still had no guarantee she wouldn't take one look at me and turn away in disgust. Maybe she would come just to have the satisfaction of spitting in my face. Did I deserve anything less?

This nap wasn't going to work, I conceded. Nervous anticipation was pumping through me like caffeine, keeping my mind from quieting. I rolled over and stared at the ceiling, my thoughts drifting to an incident in my Bible college days. . . .

"Tosini had an illegitimate kid," the student in the next booth said to his buddies. He didn't know I was sitting in the booth behind him.

"You're kidding," one of his friends said, seeming to enjoy the juicy revelation. I froze. Something cut deep into me. They continued talking back and forth about it, as if my past were some revealing television drama.

This was the place I had come to learn more about God and what was taught in the Bible. This day, though, I was learning more about the cruelty that can be inflicted by a few thoughtless words. I wished people could understand the burden I carried. Little did these potential preachers know that their words were like sharp spears, the points piercing deeply.

My cheeks grew warm, the rage pumping in my system. Someone important to me was being treated with disrespect. It was as if Heidi were being mocked for something I had done. What would happen if I stood up and looked them right in the eye? How would they feel if I showed myself and made it clear that I had overheard their malicious gossip? Would they still be so glib? What if I were just to stand up and throw their drinks in their faces, I wondered.

I didn't move, though. As the seconds passed, a sadness settled over me. I felt so isolated, so different from these people. Somehow, I thought, they must be insulated from the pain I felt, that reoccurring despair that sapped my strength like a low-grade fever. How could I fit into a religious world ruled by people like these—people who carefully followed all the rules, people who skated safely through life without ever being crippled by their own choices. How could I ever be accepted in this religious realm with the past I would always drag behind me?

How could this happen? I was devastated. I had exposed the most vulnerable place in my private world only to have my painful secret trumpeted like a headline in a grocery store tabloid. I couldn't understand. Why were people so careless and insensitive? Why did people so relish hearing of another's weaknesses? Something in me revolted that day. It would be years before I spoke another word about the girl named Heidi. . . .

I should take a shower and get cleaned up, I thought. That way I'll be ready if they come a little early. I rolled my legs over the side and sat up, noticing the pictures Holly had left behind, spread out on the bed beside me. Kneeling down, I inspected them again—Heidi grinning with a set of braces, sitting cross-legged on her school playground, tromping in the snow, stacking a collection of seashells, posing with her softball team.

Shifting my gaze from photo to photo, I considered how God had answered my prayers. This child had clearly grown up in the protective care of her heavenly Father. I hadn't known what kind of child I would meet when I had flown out here. Would she be a non-conformist, perhaps a punk-rocker with a half-shaved head or pointed jags of hair? A drug addict? A high school dropout? I was prepared to love her, whoever she was, whatever she looked like.

These photos depicted an attractive, intelligent-looking young girl. Holly had told me she had never been in serious trouble and had always done well in school. The artwork mixed in with the photos demonstrated her special artistic skills. Heidi had even been selected as one of the few students in her school to participate in an honors art program.

Holly had obviously been a devoted mother. She had parented Heidi single-handedly, holding down a full-time job during the years when there were just two of them. She had done a superb job of raising her. When Holly was working, she left Heidi in the care of Gert, a motherly middle-aged woman who lived two doors away. Gert "adopted" Heidi as part of her own family, having taken care of her since she was a newborn. She loved Heidi like her own child, baking her birthday cakes, buying her Christmas presents, and providing her with a second home and family. I marveled at how God had even provided the right person to help Holly with the so often overwhelming task of caring for a child as a single parent. And though Heidi had not grown up with all the frills of a wealthy upbringing, she had never lacked for anything. The family was better off financially than many. I shook my head in awe at the mercy of God. He heard my prayers, I thought. He cared for this child while I was absent.

My eyes latched onto a picture of Heidi when she was first born. I had missed so much, I thought. I remembered back to the time when another child of mine had entered the world . . . .

"Mr. Tosini, you can meet us in the hallway now," the nurse said, poking her head into the waiting room. "Your wife just gave birth to a little girl." Relief rushed through me, making way for the joy that followed.

When I saw that little baby, tears of awe and exhilaration swelled in my eyes. It was my birthday, and I was soon holding the best birthday present I had ever received. But as I joined Dawn in absorbing the joy of those moments, I was pierced by the thought of the birth I had not attended.

Later that morning, I headed back home to get some rest and make phone calls to family members and friends. Relaxing on the couch, I was enjoying my proud satisfaction over Jodi's arrival, yet feeling an undercurrent of despondency. The thrill of this event had made me reflect on my other little girl. Where was she now, I wondered. What would it have been like to hold her when she was so little? My questions had no answers. They just drew my attention to a painful part of me that had never healed.

A few days later, the pastor I worked with unknowingly touched that tender spot.

"Nothing like holding your first baby," he said one morning, smiling as if he knew exactly what I was feeling. "There's something so special about the first child." I smiled weakly and nodded, trying to hide my turmoil.

Why don't you tell him that you have another child out there somewhere, I said to myself, a child you have never held? What's the point? I concluded. I'm not looking for sympathy. Besides, he can't do anything about it. Nobody can but God.

That tender place inside me ached each time I witnessed a "first," those events that most parents enjoy so fully. The first steps. The first birthday party. The first successful bike ride. I cherished Jodi's and Joy's firsts, like any dad would, but each was a vivid reminder of what I had missed in another little girl's life. . . .

A car engine hummed outside the hotel room window and startled me out of my thought journey. Could it be them, I thought, looking at my watch. It was a little early still. But I jumped up to look out the fourth-floor window. The car rolled on past; I watched it turn out of the parking lot.

I might as well take a shower and get dressed, I thought. Fumbling through my suitcase, I pulled out a shirt and pair of pants. Will this be too dressy, I wondered. How will she be dressed? Is this too wrinkled, I asked myself, holding it up against my chest and examining the image in the mirror. It'll have to do.

I left my clothes on the bed and stepped into the shower stall. Shifting my head back and forth, I let the water relax my face. After I dried off, I put on the clothes I had pulled out of the suitcase. Standing in front of the mirror, I wondered if my hair could look any better. I chuckled, catching myself being more preoccupied with my appearance than usual. This must be how some girls feel, I thought, who fear their acceptance or rejection will be determined by their appearance.

I guess she'll just have to settle for the way I am, I thought. . . .

"BBBBRRRRNNNGGGGG!" My heart raced. This meant they were in the lobby, ready for me to come join them.

"Hello," I said, forcing a calmness into my tone.

"Joe?" It was Holly.

"Yes. Are you here?"

"No, we're still at home." In one rush of breath, I exhaled the air I'd been holding since the phone rang. I sat down on the bed.

"She's decided she wants to see you," Holly said. "We're leaving now, and we'll be there in fifteen minutes."

"Great," I said, starting to breathe again. "I'll see you. Good-bye." I hung up the phone.

Fifteen minutes! Fifteen minutes! What should I do when I see her? Should I give her a hug? Should I shake her hand? What will she be expecting? Will she be disappointed? What will she think of the way I look? Is she going to like me?

There was no question how I would feel about her, whether I would "like" her or not. It didn't matter what I would find. It didn't matter what she had done. None of that mattered. I just loved her.

I remembered several people asking before I came, "Do you think you're going to like her?" It was hard for anyone to understand. It was hard for them to realize that even though I didn't know her, I felt the same way about my child as they felt about theirs.

"Things like this don't always work out very well," people had cautioned me. "It's pretty late to get started now. And you have your other children, your family, another life. Don't expect anything more than a Christmas card/birthday card relationship."

I remembered listening to all these comments, knowing they were intended to cushion me from the disappointment I might face. But something inside me refused to accept them. I was determined to develop something much deeper than a Christmas card relationship, and I didn't care what the statistics might say about the odds of this working out.

Heidi would be the one to determine how things went. I knew that I wanted her as my daughter, but she was old enough to say, "No, even though you're my dad, I don't want you." She was in a position where she had to make a choice. Would she open her life to me?

All I wanted was a chance to give what I had, to express who I was to her. It didn't matter to me whether she was bright, well behaved, or had personality. I was her father. I loved her, no matter what. And I wanted desperately to tell her, and show her just that.

Standing up, I leaned against the wall by the window, my eyes fixed on the entrance to the parking lot below. It seemed that God, like a fine director of a theater production, had brought together each player in this drama in a spectacular way. It was just three weeks before that Holly's husband had knocked on the door at my parents' home. That was when I first realized that God had not forgotten about this burden I had carried all these years. He had sent Holly's husband. He had caused his job materials to be late, so that he had to wait longer than planned in New York. He had caused Holly to hold onto the address of my parents' home. He knew I needed to be in New York—that week. He had directed my friend to encourage me to attend the conference, then despite my reservations about going, had made sure I got on that flight. He knew I needed to be at my parents' home—at just the right moment. I had considered skipping my visit that afternoon, but for some reason, I had decided to make the drive. I was going to stop a few minutes at the clothing store, but that belt broke, so I had headed straight home where five minutes later the doorbell rang.

It was critical that I had answered the door. If my mother had opened the door and listened to this stranger's story, he would not have gotten a very welcoming response. It would have sounded like a wild tale to her; she may well have driven him off in such a way that they would never have tried to contact me again.

If all these factors had not synchronized perfectly, I thought, I wouldn't be sitting in this room waiting to meet the little girl—not so little now—who had occupied so much of my thoughts and emotions for the last eighteen years. No, God knew my burden. Though it often felt like I carried it alone, he had not forgotten.

I tried to decide whether I should keep looking out the window. No, I decided. I'll just sit down and wait. It didn't work. I kept getting up and peeking out, my gaze sweeping the parking lot for a particular car. I rehearsed different versions of the scene just ahead. I shake her hand. No, too impersonal. I hug her, but she pulls away. Too forward. I say hello. She smiles. Then the picture blurs; I can't tell what's going to happen. Should I be ecstatic? Or more reserved? Would I even be able to control my emotions? I had absolutely no idea what was going to happen in the next few minutes. And yet I wanted desperately for the curtain to rise on this reunion drama. This is what I'd been waiting for all these years.

What was that? A car stopped. I jumped up to the window again. It was the right car. Closing my eyes tightly, I pulled away from the window. I didn't want to see any more. Quickly, I sat back down, rigid against the back of that motel chair. Only seconds remained to map everything out. The phone would ring. I would walk down to the lobby to see her, touch her, maybe to hold her, all for the very first time.

I kept waiting. No phone call. What were they doing? Had she changed her mind? Maybe I should go down to the lobby. . . .

A sudden tapping at the door short-circuited my planning. My heart pounded furiously. Wait a minute, I thought, trying desperately to gather my thoughts. They were going to call from the lobby. Were they at the door? Or was it someone else? This wasn't the plan.

Through the peephole, I saw Holly. Looking around, I could see no one else. Heidi must be standing to the side, I reasoned. Grasping the door knob, I spun it till I heard a click, and pulled the door open.

9

THE REUNION

Through the open doorway, my eyes met Holly's, then quickly darted to the side where I saw some movement. Just then, a head peeked around the corner. It was Heidi.

"Hi," she said, smiling tentatively, squinting and shrugging her shoulders upward. Her nervousness heightened the pitch of her voice and kept her from saying anything else. All I could do was smile. Examining her quickly confirmed what the pictures had promised. Her face, though pleasant, seemed full of questions—seventeen years' worth. I wished I could have answered every one of them right there in the doorway, but in that moment of time I could answer only one.

I reached my arms out toward her. She moved closer. And we exchanged our first hug. Holly watched, and began to cry. The three of us sat down at the table, pushing the room service menu aside.

As we talked, I caught Heidi's eye for a moment. She had been looking at me intently, investigating my features, my mannerisms. As soon as my eyes met hers, though, she immediately turned away with an embarrassed giggle. I knew she was beginning to explore the countless questions she had stored up. For the first time, at age seventeen, she was looking at her real father, rather than the one she had imagined.

"Would it be okay if I held your hand?" I asked her, after a few minutes. I didn't want to overwhelm her. But I wanted her to know I was reaching out to her. Holding her hand, I thought, would communicate far more than I could say. I wanted to answer those initial questions I knew would be in her mind, "Does he want me? How does he feel about me?"

"Sure," she said.

This is a good beginning, I thought, with great relief. This child was old enough to decide whether she wanted to open the door to me. As frightening as it was to leave the decision in her hands, I could not require her to accept me. So far, she seemed willing.

"I understand you like art," I said, "and from the pictures I've been looking at, you seem to like softball and tennis, too." She smiled and nodded. "Do you know that you have two sisters?" I asked, keeping my tone as quiet and gentle as I could. Her original smile returned with an enthusiasm that lifted her eyebrows and freckled cheeks. "They sent you some letters."

"Yeah, Mom showed them to me," she said.

After a few minutes, I suggested we find some place to have dinner. We packed into Heidi's car and headed for downtown. I could tell Heidi was still nervous. When we arrived at the restaurant, she tried to swing the car smoothly into a parallel parking spot. She hit the curb, her face reddening as she had to pull out and start over.

Once inside the restaurant, a favorite of Heidi's, the three of us were seated by the front window. Holly and Heidi chose the two chairs on one side. I seated myself opposite them.

We each ordered and awaited the next development in this drama.

"Seems like a nice place," I said to Holly.

"Yes, the food's pretty good here," she replied.

"In fact this seems like a real pleasant town," I said.

"We have quite a few decent restaurants," she said.

With the introductory comments out of the way, I considered where the conversation should turn from there. Should we talk about Heidi's school? Our pasts? Was it time to mention the future? Primarily, though, I was trying to figure out what was going on in Heidi's mind. But I didn't know how to pry that door open. "Well . . ." I said, letting out a sigh, "here we are."

For a few moments, Heidi had been looking at me. I turned my eyes toward her. Up to this point, when our eyes met, she would immediately look away, nervously. This time, though, she didn't. As we exchanged that glance, I noticed her lip was quivering and tears were filling her eyes.

I tried desperately to decipher her unspoken thoughts. Was she asking where I had been all this time? Whether I had come just to ease my conscience? Or if I was expecting her to jump up and down like a child whose father just arrived home from a trip? Was she wondering if I knew how hard it had been for her not having a father? Was she wondering why she should accept me after seventeen years of silence?

What's she going to do, I wondered. Do these tears indicate her heart is softening toward me, or is she on the verge of blowing up with rage? Is she going to let out a scream and cuss me out right here in the restaurant? I couldn't tell. But within moments, Heidi lifted her arm from where it had been resting on the table. She put her hand on top of mine, wrapping her fingers around the palm of my hand, and started to cry.

That touch communicated more than I could emotionally digest. Placing her hand on mine told me that she wanted to forgive me. That single gesture showed me that whatever resentment, bitterness, or frustration she experienced for not having a father was not stronger than the desire she had to know me. It was as if love and hate had struggled together within her; her touch told me that love would win.

Until then, I had held my tears in check, though I was as emotionally fragile as I had ever been. But Heidi's tears were enough to push me beyond the bounds of control. Squeezing her hand tightly in mine, I felt emotion rising in me. It was as if the agony of the past, the joy of this moment, and the hope for the future were converging at once and bursting to the surface like the eruption of a geyser. As we waited for our dinner at that Maryland restaurant, I was helplessly overcome. I gave up the fight against my tears. And in a moment, while the other patrons enjoyed their entrees and polite conversations, the three of us wept openly. "Everything's okay," I told the waiter, when he approached to check on us. "We're just happy."

Once we all stopped crying, I knew something was different. The tears had dissolved an invisible wall of tension keeping us apart. Our journey together, to explore our pasts and anticipate our futures, had begun.

The food came in a few minutes. Holly picked up her fork but could only hold it over her plate. I, too, could only examine my food. Transporting it to my mouth seemed somehow impossible. Heidi's appetite, though, seemed perfectly intact. She grabbed her fork and slipped bite after bite into her mouth.

With a now apparent enthusiasm about me, Heidi asked her mom if she could skip school the next day. Fully understanding the significance of the occasion, Holly quickly approved. "Do you think you could stay an extra day?" Heidi asked me, after she had finished her dinner. I had planned to return after just a day in Maryland.

"Sure, that would be great," I said, delighted and relieved by the interest she was showing in me. With the vigor of a child anticipating a trip to Disneyland, Heidi began mapping out the next day's journey to the landmarks of her past.

"Mom, can you give me a quarter?" Heidi said, remembering that she needed to let her friends know she wouldn't be driving to school in the morning. Holly reached for her purse.

"Wait a minute," I said, reaching into my pocket. "Take this, Heidi," I said, holding a coin out toward her. "Here's the first quarter your father has ever given you."

After dinner we strolled down the street, holding hands. Heidi directed us up a flight of stairs to a restaurant where her close friend worked. Heidi was eager to break the news about our reunion. As we approached her friend, I wondered how Heidi would introduce me. How would it sound, I wondered, to hear her refer to me as her father. Or would she just introduce me as "Joe"? I wasn't sure.

As we approached her friend, she didn't hesitate. "This is my father," Heidi exclaimed enthusiastically to her classmate, with the owner standing alongside. I smiled at Heidi's friend, then noticed the man looking at me. I wondered what thoughts he was hiding behind that silent, staring gaze. Was he wondering where I'd been all this time? Was he trying to solve in his own mind the mystery of the last seventeen years?

Outside again, Holly ran into a friend and began to chat. Heidi and I walked on ahead. We stopped at the corner, waiting for Holly. I reached out and pulled Heidi toward me. My eyes found hers. "Heidi, I love you," I told her. "I want to know you." A short time later, we drove back to the motel and said our first-day good-byes.

"I'd like you to meet my father," Heidi said the next day to a man my age, also named Joe. The father of one of her close friends, Joe was someone who had had a close view of Heidi's adolescent years and had shown her kindness. Heidi seemed so proud to introduce me as her father, as if some burden had been removed, some shame wiped away with one stroke. Joe's eyes lit up and a smile swept across his face as he shook my hand vigorously. His wife had not seen her father for more than twenty years, so this family grasped the significance of this day more than many could.

Though Heidi wasn't saying this, I sensed a process had begun where she was feeling more complete as a person, with a clearer sense of her own identity. Children look to their fathers; Heidi was beginning to look to me.

We left her friend's house and began making the rounds: to Heidi's school, then to her baby-sitter's house. As we drove, she filled me in on more of the missing years. We were both more comfortable talking about the past. The present was still a little awkward; the future still up in the air.

"Come on, let me get a picture of you two," Heidi insisted, at the table where Holly, Heidi, and I had come for dinner. I had bought Heidi a camera, and we had been putting it to good use all day. I wanted pictures to take home to Dawn, Jodi, and Joy, and my other friends, to begin introducing them to Heidi. Just like when a baby is born, I wanted a picture of everything, even though this baby of mine was a senior in high school. Holly had also been eager to get several pictures of Heidi with her father. Now it was Heidi's turn. "Move in a little bit," she said, wanting to frame the picture just right.

As Holly and I struck this pose, though, I had to superimpose a smile on my unhappy thought. As I leaned toward Holly, I realized that this was the first time Heidi had ever seen her parents together. Her childhood years lacked the strength of a two-parent family; she had been denied the full dose of affection and support that every child needs. It had been our selfishness in those California days, our blind determination to pursue our own pleasures that had brought this about. Heidi had deserved a better welcome on her arrival into the world than the half-family we had arranged.

I was sure I could read some of the questions occupying Heidi's mind. Up to this point, she knew next to nothing about her parents as a young couple. Had they been married? Had they cared at all about each other? Why hadn't they stayed together? It wasn't time yet for Heidi to pose these questions; nor was it time for them to be answered. What grieved me was that this young girl had to be saddled with questions like these at all. These were matters she should not have had to be concerned with. As these thoughts were running through my mind, I was wrestling with the sadness of it all.

"Good morning."

"Good morning. Did you sleep well?" I asked Heidi, climbing into Holly's little Triumph Spitfire. A bit of awkwardness had crept back into our conversation, since we had said our good-byes the night before. On this third day on my Maryland trip, the day I was to leave, this was our first time out alone. Holly had felt it would be good for father and daughter to spend a few hours together.

Heidi had picked out a restaurant for our breakfast meeting. By this time I was starting to get my appetite back, especially since I'd been too strung out to eat much over the last two days. We both ordered omelets, and I mentioned how I was looking forward to satisfying the growl in my stomach. But as the waiter set down our orders, I began to get concerned. I cut through my omelet and tried to pick up a bite. As I lifted the fork, the under-cooked yoke was dripping steadily toward my plate. I put my fork down; suddenly my appetite wasn't so acute. Heidi was embarrassed since she had picked this restaurant to make this first father-daughter outing special.

I assured her I had more important things on my mind than orange juice and omelets. This was to be the day for some serious discussions about present realities and future possibilities. The last two days were easier, stepping back into the past. Now came the hard part: looking toward the future. Since this would be our last day together in Maryland, Heidi, too, was eager to explore some more sensitive issues with me.

"Well, Heidi, tell me about yourself. . . . Tell me what you think about . . . how you feel about things. . . ." I said, just wanting to begin drawing out some of the information hidden inside her that would help me piece together a fuller picture of who this daughter of mine really was. "There may be a lot of things about me you may want to know," I added. "I want you to feel free to ask me questions, and I'll try my best to answer them." We talked for a few minutes at the table, just beginning to explore this new territory. Then we left the restaurant and got back in the car.

I watched her lower herself behind the steering wheel of this little sports car. As she turned the key in the ignition, it occurred to me that here I was watching her drive a car; I had never even seen her ride a bike. I had missed so much. How could I make up for those precious years?

We went to a park where she used to play as a little girl. This was the place Holly had taken Heidi countless times over the years to swing, picnic, and feed the ducks. This special place brought back warm memories.

Heidi saw a friend there and again introduced me as her father. The woman was stunned; she had known Heidi for several years and was aware her father was not a part of her life. Heidi handed the woman her camera, and there we were posing for yet another picture. It was like walking into the pages of a fairy tale, a father finding his lost child, almost too good to be true.

She showed me some more sights and introduced me to more friends along the way. Then while we were driving in the car, she made a proclamation: "You know, I'm kind of old now," she said. "I don't need a dad anymore. I think it would be really good for us to be friends."

I didn't say anything for a few moments. "You don't need a dad, huh?" I replied, a little concerned but not panicking. I figured I'd just give it some time and see what happened. I knew I couldn't push her.

Throughout the day we talked often of her coming to Missouri to visit. I told her all about Dawn, Jodi, and Joy, about the church, about our neighborhood, and about the town I live in. Especially after reading the letters, she was eager to come.

It was hard to say good-bye after that three-day stay. So much had happened in such a short time as we began reliving our separate journeys. But there was so much more to say, so much more to do. We agreed on a time for both Holly and Heidi to come to Missouri for their first visit—in about two weeks.

At the airport, my farewell was dramatically different from my arrival. Heidi walked me to the counter to get my ticket, and the three of us sat down to wait the few minutes before boarding. Holly was flashing pictures of Heidi and me, as we laughed and talked together, holding hands and hugging each other playfully. After an uncertain beginning, none of us knowing for sure how the weekend would go, we all regretted it was ending so soon. At the same time, we knew that our journey together had only begun.

After a few minutes, the flight attendant issued the boarding call. "I'll see you soon," I said, hugging each of them.

After I boarded the plane, I pulled out a letter Holly had handed me while we were waiting. She had typed it, she told me, amid many tears while Heidi and I had been out together earlier in the day:

> *Dear Dawn, Jodi, Joy, and Joe,*
> *These few days have been the most joyous in eighteen years. It has been such an unbelievable happening that has occurred and brought these years to a complete circle. Your overwhelming love and faith that you have extended to us and to so many others really cannot be described in words. . . .*

We are really looking forward to coming to Columbia, and I really wish that we started last night and might be halfway there by now. I have such a strong yearning to see everything that Joe has spoken to us of the fellowship. Even as I write this, I have great pain in my heart (tears) to be there with you. I have reread your most kind notes and reviewed your pictures so many times in this short time, and I cherish them beyond belief. . . .

Hopefully we can all get together very soon—either in Missouri or Maryland. . . . It is 11:32 a.m. this Saturday morning, and I am expecting Heidi and Joe back from town shortly. I really wished to be with them this morning as this visit has been so short but so very dear to us. I'm really feeling so sad because he will be gone in a few hours—not out of our lives, only a little ways away but still in our minds and heart so very much. And with that image that we carry of him is you, Dawn, Joy and Jodi. The pain is really immense—it's like being thrown a life-line in waves of ocean and being so fearful of not being saved.

These few days have been such a miracle we don't wish it to end. I know, however, that it really has just begun. I turned over and prayed to God last night for the first time in a very very long time. . . . This contact, this miracle of the last few weeks has been like a rebirth in life—I really cannot describe it. To think until two weeks ago we had no knowledge of the four of you in Columbia, that we may be a part of—and to now know that we are attached is very touching. I feel so much pain for not having it before. . . .

This has appeared to be such a dream, however we must keep pinching our minds, for this is really happening. There really are no words to really describe it. It is just so marvelous to look at each other. I have just so enjoyed watching Heidi and Joe's profiles—the similarities. Their smiles, their tears, their laughs, their silence, silence of amazement.

I cannot and never will be able to thank you, Dawn, Joy,

Jodi enough for sharing your father and husband with us these few days. It is most generous of you in your hearts to include us. The thoughts, questions, wondering, worrying of all these years has finally been answered. The joy of Heidi and Joe finding each other and now having a whole new family to think and pray for is just unexplainable. . . .

This miracle . . . has opened up a whole new world for all of us and we have now a whole new life to share with each other. No time is soon enough for us to all get together and see and feel each other and our love.

I want you to know that you are in our minds forever, and the future is going to be quite an experience to behold.

> *So very, very much love,*
> *God bless you all,*
> *Holly & Heidi*

GOD WEEPS

My mind couldn't rest. As the plane flew over Pennsylvania, I kept seeing Heidi's face, examining each feature, remembering her mannerisms, the way she spoke. I played back in my mind scenes of precious hours we had had together over those two days, reliving the conversations, the glances, the feeling of her hand clasping mine.

This is just like having a baby, I thought, only this one is seventeen.

My mind jumped ahead a day, and I pictured myself in front of the congregation, telling people for the first time about Heidi's existence. I would be back in the environment where I carried the responsibility of pastoring nearly a thousand people. These people looked to me to help them sort out the key issues in life, to help them understand the message of the Bible, to help them grasp the purpose God had for them.

How could I possibly recount to them the emotional storm I had been through these past few weeks, even these past eighteen years—longer than any of them had known me? Many, of course, would understand the thoughtless frivolity that young people sometimes display, exploring lifestyles they only later recognize as destructive. But how many of them would be able to identify with a person—their pastor, no less—who had fathered a child he had never known? How would they react? How would I tell them? Would I be able to communicate my story in a way that could benefit their lives?

As I searched for the words that I would share, I pulled my Bible out of my briefcase. An image crossed my mind of David and

Jonathan, so I turned to the book of First Samuel, where their friendship is described.

David, a lowly shepherd's son, had become a warrior in the king's army, and felt a strong kinship with King Saul's son, Jonathan. The Bible describes David, who became one of the great kings of Israel, as "a man after God's own heart." David and Jonathan were united in heart and mind and became the closest of friends, even to the point of making a covenant. This pact, a pledge that David would support and defend Jonathan and his family in the face of any threat, linked them with bonds even closer than natural blood ties. This commitment went beyond the grave: the two promised that if one died, the survivor would care for the other's household.

Events in David's life had come to a climax. It had been God's sovereign choice to appoint him as king in place of Saul. Jonathan, who had a natural right to the throne, graciously welcomed David's appointment as from God. But Saul resented David deeply and clung to his power. Ruled by selfish ambition, he was even prepared to kill David to protect his position.

David barely escaped one murder attempt, and he had to flee to avoid another violent confrontation with Saul. So the day came when Jonathan and David knew they would be seeing each other for the last time.

I had read the story many times before. But this time, as I flew home, remembering the pain of my past, the story took on a fresh meaning.

Jonathan and David both experienced the hurt resulting from the conflict with the king. Indeed, they would both suffer the repercussions for the rest of their lives. But they did not experience the pain to the same degree. As they embraced for the last time, the story reads, "they wept together, but David more so."

Jonathan loved David like a brother and grieved deeply over this tragedy that was befalling them. But David—the man after God's own heart, the biblical character most closely identified with Jesus—wept more.

Suddenly, a truth set off a charge inside me. My mind went back to the pain I'd felt. I had especially grieved over a girl who faced a fatherless future because of me. I had cried out to God, pleading with Him to care for this child I would be powerless to care for myself. But then, sitting in that airplane, I realized something about God. It was so easy to see him as an angry God of judgment. But I was moved by the revelation that God was more hurt than angry over my wrongs, and that the grief he felt was greater than mine.

Like Jonathan, I had wept over the pain of my life. But like David, Jesus had wept more. I had grieved over my mistakes; he had grieved more. I had agonized over a little girl who would have no father to protect and guide her; God felt even more anguish. I wanted more than anything to shield that child from the dangers that awaited her in a cruel world; Jesus desired her protection even more.

God, I realized, was affected by my distress. He felt my pain, and it touched him, moved him, hurt him. He suffered alongside me and shouldered my sorrows.

This, indeed, was a tender-hearted God. He felt deep emotion for his children. He was a father more motivated than I to nurture a little girl whom He knew perfectly well. He had responded to my prayer by putting an umbrella of protection around his child, to preserve her physically, emotionally, and spiritually.

As I remembered seeing Heidi in the pictures spread out on that motel room bed, and then in the doorway peeking around the corner, I realized that it was no accident that she had grown up with a baby-sitter who cared for her like a second mother, and with a wholesome friend whose father offered her parent-like care. I realized it was no accident that she had been protected in her relationships with young men, sheltered from the scars of immorality. I realized God had given her artistic skill, which provided her an outlet of expression as she explored her adolescent world.

God had been right alongside Heidi every mile of her journey. So many times I had come to feel that I carried this burden alone, felt that no other person could understand the pain that wracked my spirit. But on that airplane, I realized for the first time that there was another person who felt my pain, only more deeply still. There was another person who cared even more for Heidi than I did. I had wept over my calamity, over my secret pain, but Jesus had wept more.

As I folded my handkerchief, I was satisfied that God had given me the words to offer the congregation the next day. I knew that as I looked out on the room full of faces—some young, some old, some battered by life more than others—they would all have their own stories to tell. They would all be carrying their own pain. They would all have cried their own tears.

Now not only could I share my own story of tragedy and restoration, but I could also encourage them with this new realization—that as life unfolds with its disappointments and heartaches, God cares more about our calamities than we do. It may not seem like it all the time. God may sometimes be taking care of things quietly behind the scenes, but he does not forget us. He does not leave us to bear the burdens of life alone.

Tomorrow I would tell them: they have wept, but God has wept more.

SECTION TWO:

RESTORATION

SUNDAY MORNING

"Be sure to be here on Sunday," one of the leaders had told the congregation at our Friday night meeting. "Joe has an extremely important announcement, and he wants to be sure everyone is here." That set the congregation abuzz, wondering what I would say.

Sunday morning the thrill of our reunion and gratitude over the airplane revelation was still rushing through me. I was about to open up some of the most tender areas of my heart to the church. How would they react? What would they say? Would I even be able to get through the story? Hardly an hour had gone by since I'd left Maryland that I hadn't had to reach for tissues to deal with a surge of emotion.

We began the service in the usual way, with a series of worship choruses that spoke of the love, mercy, and strength of God. The hour or so we spent worshipping gave me a chance to quiet my mind, to concentrate on God's goodness, and to reflect on the miracle of these last few days.

As we prepared to move on in the meeting, the worship leader invited everyone to listen as a chorus of thirty-five men and women presented a song drawn in part from Psalm 103. I was touched by how appropriate it seemed.

> *He will not always accuse*
> *But will graciously excuse*
> *All our sins and our iniquities*

The Lord is compassionate
The Lord is gracious
Slow to anger
Abounding with love[1]

Somehow it seemed that this psalm set the stage for the story the congregation was about to hear. As I listened, I observed their faces. This story could only be understood, I thought, by those who have experienced the mercy of God, by people who know God doesn't relate to us based on how well we have performed.

I felt ready to step to the podium and begin. As I faced the group, I was overwhelmed with the dedication many of these people had displayed over the years. More than a decade before, a handful of eager college students had set out to establish a church family where love for God and for one another meant something. I was proud of how far we'd come together.

"Some of you may be wondering what in the world I'm going to talk about this morning," I said, adjusting my microphone. "Is anybody wondering that?"

"I will probably have a difficult time maintaining my emotions," I warned them, "but I'll do my best to pull myself together. The last two weeks have been an emotional time in my life, in my family's life. I don't have the words to describe what has transpired in the last few days, but I will tell you it is really good."

The room was completely silent. Every face I saw showed concern.

"I prayed for a passage of Scripture that I could share with you this morning, and this is the verse that came to me on the airplane home yesterday." Opening my Bible to First Samuel, I read the story of Jonathan and David, concluding with the phrase that had touched me so deeply on the airplane: ". . . and they kissed each other and wept together, but David more so."

Knowing the majority of people listening were going to be in for a shock, I took a deep breath and said, "Let's go back to Berkeley, California in 1968, where I was living at that time. Those were pretty wild days, you know. During that time I had a relationship with a woman. And one day she informed me she was expecting a baby."

The bomb had been dropped. The silence, and the concern, remained. I told them the woman had left for the East Coast and called only once, to tell me a girl was born and to give me the child's name.

No one in this group, except Dawn, had known me in those days. Only a handful of people here had known about Heidi before this. This congregation had known me only as their pastor, though I had talked at times about the night in California when Jesus revealed himself to me. "This circumstance helped push me to a place of desperation where I cried out to God, wanting to know what in the world life was all about," I said. "Right after that, Dawn and I were married. Both of us have carried the weight of this for eighteen years." I began to notice a few teary eyes in the sea of faces; I was keeping my tissues close at hand.

"There hasn't been a week go by in eighteen years that I have not thought about. . ."

My voice started to crack; the emotional floodwaters were rising again. Pulling away from the podium, I had to wait a few moments for the wave to pass before I could talk again. I took a breath and wiped the tears.

". . . a little girl named Heidi."

By now some people were sobbing openly. Tears trickled down many faces, but everyone was still rapt with attention. I thought about how I had listened to so many of them tell their stories about the pain in their lives. "People have said to me, 'Joe, you could never understand certain things about me because your life seems to go so well.' And so many times I've had to bite my tongue, because I know what it's like to carry a pain. And Dawn knows what it is like to carry pain."

I then began explaining the events that had overtaken us: about going to New York for the conference I hadn't even wanted to attend, about the car breaking down enroute to Long Island, and all the circumstances that led to that startling encounter at the front door of my parents' home.

I tried to convey that God leads us even when we're not aware of it. I wanted them to understand the depth of this miracle, and I recounted the many factors that had to come together perfectly in order for this remarkable reunion to take place. "We can call it chance, call it coincidence, or we can call it the hand of God."*

The other leaders had offered unanimous support through these weeks. "We've got quite a family here," I said, turning around and glancing at each of the men who were with me on the platform. "Every one of these men was emotionally comforting to me. . . . We rejoice together, and we weep together. . . . I can't say enough for the leaders who stand with me."

They also needed to know how my own family had handled the news. "You know, kids are kids, but I've got great kids," I said, looking down at the row where Dawn, Jodi, and Joy were sitting. "Jodi and Joy were just tremendous. I knew Dawn would be tremendous, too. She has been praying for Heidi all these years."

In the midst of this most serious explanation, it occurred to me that some people might be there for the first time. I couldn't resist lightening things up a bit. "By the way, for those of you who are visiting this morning, this isn't a normal service. . . ."

From there, I told them of how Heidi had grown up without a father. Prayer after prayer had been answered over the years, I continued. "Every time we'd pray for the children, we'd always pray for three, although one was never mentioned openly. We'd just say, 'Lord, protect her, help her.' "

Once I got to the part about actually meeting Heidi, only four days before, a smile began to replace my tears. Telling the story again helped me remember each detail. I started with my first conversation with Holly at the park in Maryland, then told of the first encounter with Heidi at the door of my motel room.

"We just sort of walked around and fell in love with each other," I said. I told the congregation I had spent quite a bit of time talking to Holly and Heidi about the church, about my own relationship with Jesus, and about our people-oriented lifestyle. "They are just overwhelmed. I wanted to bring them yesterday, but they will be here

---

*Someone later factored in the several circumstances that had to coincide for my "chance" meeting with Holly's husband to take place that day at my parents' home. After his calculations, he concluded that the odds of that meeting happening by chance were 1 in 500 billion.

in two weeks." At that announcement, I heard that familiar noise that comes from hundreds of people reacting simultaneously. I saw smiles and knew the news was well received.

I wanted to prepare the people a bit for Holly and Heidi's arrival, so I read several portions of the letter she sent back with me, a letter I had first read myself only the day before on the airplane home. "Heidi's mother has really been touched, obviously, and she just wants Heidi and me to be close." With that, I began recounting the insights that had come to me the previous day about Jonathan and David. Over the years, many people in the church had shared painful portions of their lives with me. I wanted to see them helped, and I hoped this story would assist them in the healing process.

"I wept over this situation for eighteen years," I told them, "but Jesus has wept more. He weeps more over your sin than you do. Your problem, your shame, that secret regret you keep in your heart— Jesus feels your deepest hurt and cares more about redeeming your wrongs than you do. The Bible is a book of restoration, a book about taking that which is lost and bringing it to where it can be found . . . God was faithful to me, and he's going to be faithful to you."

At that point, I turned the meeting over to Bob, the oldest member of our leadership team and a father of nine children. "As a father, I am very touched. . . ." He stopped momentarily as his own tears began. Bob said he felt God wanted to use my relationship with Heidi to show individuals in the congregation how much God desires to restore the damage in their past.

"We should be praying as never before," he said. "There are those here who live with a tragic situation and long to see God do something wonderful," he said. "For those, there is great hope. I know a number of people whose lives were in ruin, people who could not see any reason for their existence. I've seen God pull their lives together. . . ."

He concluded on a note of enthusiasm. "We're so happy for the restoration taking place in this family, and earnestly desire God's blessing upon them."

After Bob stepped away from the podium, I returned, moved by his comments and the clear support coming from the congregation. "I don't believe that God wants just to minister to me and my family,"

I said. "He wants to reach out to help all of us. He doesn't perform a miracle just for one person, or two, or three. He can put faith in your heart where you don't have it right now. God can begin healing you today."

My "miracle" wasn't just for Heidi and me. God was using my story to penetrate the hearts of many others. I mentioned there might be some girls there who had never felt a father's love, or men who, for whatever reason, had been separated from a child. So many thoughts were running through my mind of the relational scars that people often carry for a lifetime, the emotional wounds of abuse, divorce, estrangement, or a lost love.

Another one of the leaders tapped my shoulder and indicated he had something he wanted to say. He directed his comments toward those who carried a heavy load of guilt from past mistakes. "I believe some of you feel so ashamed that you don't want to expose to God what you've done. Well," he continued, "God knows all about you. The love of God is so extensive, there is nothing about you that can shock him. . . . Just let him love you."

Over the next several days, I was flooded with letters, phone calls, and comments offering support and encouragement to me as my story continued to unfold. Several letters and conversations indicated that deep healing had come to people who had suffered from hidden pain of their own.

One man in the church, a powerfully built weight-lifter, told me he had been profoundly affected by my story. To my surprise, he handed me a poem he had written about his little girl, from whom he had been separated. The poem was titled "Rachel":

> *Oh little girl, my heart does sing*
> *Where are you today?*
> *Sitting in the backyard swing?*
> *Have you gone to play?*

Did I fix your hair just right,
Did I make you smile?
Did I warn that some dogs bite,
Did I hold you for a while?

Oh little girl, the sky is blue,
Clear now for you to see
How deeply that I love you
And want you close to me.

The swing moves only by the wind;
Your toys are want for wear.
I see places where you have been,
And only you were there.

Paint with colors that fill your dreams,
Show the world that you care.
My little girl grew up it seems,
Even though I wasn't there.

Oh little girl, my heart does sing
Where are you today?
Sitting in the backyard swing?
Have you gone to play?

— Dad

1. Lyrics from "Bless the Lord, O My Soul," Copyright © 1985 Mike Herron. Used by permission.

12

DESTINATION: RESTORATION

Everyone loves fairy tales. Life would have been so simple if this story could have stayed on that level. I had found the long-lost child. She had found her dad. The whole world is happy. And we would just smile at each other the rest of our lives.

The truth is that beneath our conversation and lingering in each other's minds were a thousand questions casting shadows of doubt on the future. How could either of us know whether this relationship story would have a good ending? How could we know that what had started out like a fairy tale wouldn't take a terrible twist and turn into a nightmare?

Standing at the emotional peak of our recent reunion, I could look into the distance, where our journey would continue. I was still enjoying the thrill that had lifted us to the mountaintop, but I could now see the perils that might beset us as we pressed forward.

After all these years, would Heidi be able to adjust to the presence of a father in her life? Would the bitterness that would surely emerge overpower the hope of a healthy relationship? Would she be able to face questions that had no answers: Why did she have to be born the way she had been? Why did she have to grow up without a father?

I wondered how this major event would affect my life. What changes would I have to make now since I would be responsible for a young girl facing the transition into her college years? Could I handle it if, all of a sudden, she were to say to me, "I don't want to see you anymore"? What if my enthusiasm were to wane and, God forbid, I would ever say to myself, "I wish this meeting had never happened"? Do I have any assurance this reunion would have a positive outcome? The questions frightened me; I didn't know the answers.

As if these concerns relating directly to Heidi and me weren't enough, many more questions emerged about the role of the large supporting cast in this drama. People had responded wonderfully so far. The reunion between Heidi and me had gained the full support of family and friends. Everyone was excited and hopeful for the future. But their initial response would be tested as the road we were traveling became more difficult, the journey more hazardous.

How would Dawn handle this new entry into her life? I wondered how she would be affected by my intense interest in Heidi and whether she would agree with my decisions as I carried out my responsibilities as her father.

And Jodi and Joy would surely react to my excitement about getting to know this new teenager in my life. Would they be jealous of the attention directed toward Heidi? Would some kind of sibling rivalry ultimately overwhelm the joy of finding a new sister?

And beyond my own family, I thought about the church, the hundreds of families who had looked to me for leadership. How would they handle this? Would they remain as willing to embrace Heidi as they did the rest of my family? Would their view toward me be tainted by my public admission of a child who was born outside of marriage?

And then there was Holly. She had invested the prime years of her life providing for Heidi, loving her, caring for her. Would she be able to be supportive of me entering her daughter's life? Or would her initial enthusiasm wear thin, tempting her to yearn for the yesterday when she was the only parent Heidi knew?

As I pondered how we would progress through these troublesome places, many caring, well-meaning people offered advice about what steps to take, which paths to avoid. "Be cautious," some would say. "Don't move too fast. And don't be disappointed if the relationship doesn't move far beyond the getting acquainted stage."

"Keep your relationship on more of a distant level," I would hear.

"Don't try to make her like your other kids."

Some feared the worst. "Your wife's not going to handle it. Your kids aren't going to handle it. Heidi's not going to handle it. You're not going to handle it. It's all going to blow up, and it'll all be over."

Often, as I filtered through the advice and pondered the potential dangers being addressed, I found no peace in heeding the warnings. Those possibilities disturbed me at times. But oddly though, I seemed to have a kind of internal compass guiding me, choosing the way for me, indicating which moves to make, which turns to take.

"Please take my advice," one person told me. "Be happy you met her. Be happy you can have some sort of communication with her and be involved with her somehow for the rest of her life. But don't think you can start over now and get to the point where she feels like you're the father she never had. If you expect that kind of relationship, then you're going to end up disappointed."

Well, I had enjoyed getting acquainted with Heidi. But despite the questions, despite the dangers, despite the sacrifices required from everyone involved, my course was fixed. The destination I had in mind lay well beyond getting acquainted, well beyond being "happy I had met her," well beyond having "some sort of communication." My heart was set on a miracle: restoration.

I wanted to claim my rightful place in her life, and I wanted Heidi to have her rightful place in mine. I could be the father that I was supposed to be to her, and she could be the daughter she was supposed to be to me. Somehow, whether it was comfortable or not, the other players would have to fit into that arrangement, and in the end, I believed, everyone would be happier we did it this way.

When I get myself set in a certain direction, it's hard for me to change. So I will admit that much of the advice I received during this early stage fell on somewhat deaf ears. It wasn't that I didn't appreciate the concern. But often it simply would not have brought me to the goal I was determined to reach.

When people would caution me to go slowly with Heidi, to not expect too much response from her, I thought about a parent bringing a baby back from the hospital. Who would say to that parent,

"Be cautious. Don't be overly protective. Don't give the child too much attention"? That would be absurd. That new parent is going to lavish affection on that child as the initial bonding process takes place. A parent has certain automatic responses to a child. These emotional reflexes are impossible to ignore.

During the initial months of our reunion, I was an emotional wreck. Our first meeting and the first few steps along the path toward restoration carved out my emotional capacities to new depths. I cried, laughed, and dreamed more than I ever had in my life. I was so preoccupied that I had trouble concentrating on the daily business at hand, and my behavior was enough to drive most everyone around me out of their minds. But it all seemed to be part of the journey I had to take, and I didn't feel inclined to fight it.

People around me could have tried to analyze the emotional process I was going through. They could break it down and identify the reasons I was feeling and behaving this way—guilt, love, fear, hope, anxiety—explaining that mixing these ingredients together would produce the experiences I was having.

But understanding the dynamics of my experience wasn't all that important to me; I couldn't seem to make any emotional adjustments anyway. Exercising control over my responses hardly seemed possible. It was as if I had started jogging down a steep incline, and once I started down the hill, I couldn't slow my pace. All I could do was try to stay on my feet and keep moving forward.

I was fully aware I was going for something that was difficult. I wanted this girl to call me dad, wanted her to have my name, Tosini. I wanted her to understand my faith and to know the heavenly father who had cared for her when I wasn't there.

It was my desire to influence the decisions she would make, the road she would choose, the people she would link herself with. My aim was to support her, completely. I wanted her to have a healthy dependence on her father and a security in his protection and love. I wanted her to know and love Dawn and to be bonded with Jodi and Joy as sisters.

I wanted there to be respect and care between her mother and me.

My parents ought to know their granddaughter, I reasoned; they loved their other grandchildren dearly, and Heidi should have the same relationship. I wanted the rest of my family to accept her and the church to take her in and love her, too.

It was my conviction that the world ought to know it was possible to fuse two severed lives. Others who have buried the pain of broken relationships need to know that God can take care of their private circumstances that lie beyond their control. My hopes were high, but I was looking for the miracle of a fully restored relationship. And I would be disappointed by anything less.

13

DAD

Some three months had passed since our reunion when Heidi joined us at my parent's house in New York for Christmas. It was her first chance to meet all my relatives—cousins, uncles, aunts—a big crowd, all talking and gesturing Italian-style. It was a stimulating weekend for a girl who grew up with a small, relatively reserved family.

On the flight back to Missouri, where we planned to usher in the new year together, I looked over and noticed she was crying.

"What's the matter?" I asked.

She was quiet at first. Finally she told me.

"I don't feel right calling you 'Joe'," she said. "But I'll never be able to call you 'Dad' either." It was then, for the first time, that Heidi opened up and told me of the pain that had shrouded her past as she faced her world without a father. Heidi had known almost nothing about me until a few weeks before we met. Through the years, she had speculated that perhaps her mother and father had been married and that her father had left—not wanting a child. She wondered why, after all this time, they had never heard from him. Maybe he was dead. She didn't know. Something must have happened, she thought, something so bad her mom wanted to protect her from the knowledge. The awkwardness and the prolonged silence seemed to indicate that the topic of her father brought back bad memories. Heidi concluded it was probably best not to do any digging, but to leave it buried where it had always been and learn to live with it.

By the time she turned seventeen, it was easier for Heidi and her mother to talk about certain subjects. It was then, in the summer of 1986, that the long silence was broken. Heidi and her mom were together enjoying a sunny afternoon, driving around looking for an antique shop. Through some turn of the conversation Holly began describing what Heidi's father looked like. Heidi had known his background was Italian, but she was surprised to learn he had dark hair and olive skin since she had auburn hair and a fair complexion. Then, she heard the name for the first time: Joe . . . Joe Tosini.

The thought struck her that she might have had that last name. "How do you spell that?" she asked. Hearing the answer, she wrote the letters in the air with her finger, trying to imagine what the name looked like.

"What's he doing now?" Heidi ventured.

"He's probably a pilot, living in California or New York," Holly replied. "I've been thinking about this lately, Heidi. . . maybe the time has come to try to look him up."

As Heidi and I continued talking in the airplane, her mind flipped back through the years, retracing scenes sketched in her memory. . . .

A man her mom had been dating came by one day while Heidi was playing on the porch with a neighbor. Her mom was working nearby in the flower bed.

Heidi was five years old, old enough to be aware that her other friends had men in their lives they called "Dad." She felt the gap in her family and wanted to fit this man into it. Perhaps he was her real father, she thought.

Pointing at the man who had walked up, she said, "That's my dad," to her friend, loud enough so that her mom and the man could hear. It took much courage for her to say those words.

They both looked over at her. Heidi waited nervously to see if her hopes would be confirmed. The man's surprised look showed genuine concern but not the warm acceptance for which Heidi had hoped. Rather than coming over to her and embracing her as his daughter, he looked away and resumed his conversation. Heidi then realized all her wishing hadn't made her dream come true. This man was not her father.

About two years later, Heidi was playing a game with neighborhood kids. All the players locked their arms together and tried to keep the boy who was "it" from breaking through. The boy eyed the spot on the line where he thought he had the best chance. He ran full speed toward Heidi and crashed against her arm. He broke through easily, leaving Heidi's arm limp from the collision.

The other kids, especially two tough-acting boys, started teasing her, mocking her in front of the others.

"You're lousy. You can't play," they chided. "Go home, little girl."

Amid her tears, she had to gasp for air, her tension tightening her airway. She stumbled her way home, crying uncontrollably. Even when she arrived, she couldn't calm down and continued to hyperventilate.

How she wished there was someone to run to who could defend her against those cruel kids. How she wished for a father to protect her, like her other friends had. She tried to calm down, but she felt utterly defenseless, vulnerable to a too often heartless world.

The glaring light blinded her as the dentist crouched over her, peering inside her mouth.

"Looks like you may be ready for braces before long," said the dentist, a warm man who showed all the signs of a prosperous life. Heidi was about twelve and visiting the dentist she, as well as Holly and her husband, had seen regularly for years. She couldn't respond because his hand was holding an instrument inside her mouth.

"Where did you get these teeth?" he asked, commenting on the gap between her front teeth. "Your mom doesn't have teeth like this. Do you have your father's teeth?"

"Well, I think it's a mix between my grandfather's and my dad's," Heidi said, as soon as he moved his hand. She felt the anxiety rising, as it did anytime someone began to get too inquisitive about her family history. She had tried to calculate an answer that would stop the questioning. She couldn't resort to her normal response, which was to present her mom's husband as her father. The dentist knew him and probably knew he wasn't her real father.

"Where does your dad live?" he asked, in a friendly tone.

There it was. The line of questioning she dreaded the most. Her mind raced to find a way out. The hygienist and dental assistant were standing beside the dentist. It seemed all three were staring at her behind their surgical masks, awaiting her explanation of her missing dad.

"I don't know right now," she said, unable to think of a way to sidestep the question or redirect the conversation.

With the stark fluorescent light still glaring in her eyes, she wished she could be anywhere but in that dental chair under this interrogation. Despite her discomfort, the man wouldn't stop. His curiosity kept driving him.

"Do you see him much?" he asked.

Why can't he mind his own business? Heidi thought, wondering if he had ever asked her mom about this. How much does he know?

"No," she said simply, answering his question. Her voice shook slightly as her face burned red.

She thought about how this man had such a "normal" family, a wife and kids, and a successful lifestyle. He must think I'm so odd, she thought, such a misfit. She couldn't read his expression behind his mask, but she suspected a look of condescension.

Heidi went on to tell me of more incidents that had periodically underscored the fact that half her roots were missing. Every time a form needed to be filled out, she would always be afraid the person collecting it would notice the line was blank where her father's name was supposed to go. Heidi developed an entire repertoire of excuses about why her father wasn't around. They're divorced. He's on a business trip. He doesn't live with me. Most of the time her web of lies and half-truths shielded her from the judgments of those around her. Periodically, though, someone would see through her manufactured stories, and her fatherlessness would be exposed. She would always try to hide her sense of shame.

One time, she had to diagram her family tree as a class project, showing every detail of her blood line. She feared her teacher and her classmates would notice that the father side of her tree was filled by her step-father and his kids from another marriage. She hoped nobody would ask any questions about her family, so she could slide through the project without being exposed.

Heidi told me of her underlying insecurity, her sense of inadequacy that resulted from not knowing her father. She felt like an outcast, abnormal, like she was in a class of people inferior to everyone else. No one she knew could understand what it would be like to walk in her shoes.

Heidi told me that she began developing a hardness trying to cope with her fatherlessness, a harsh attitude toward men in general. She had simply never related closely with men, she said. The philosophies of the women's movement clicked inside her as she reached her high school years and adapted to an adult world. Never wanting a family, she was baffled by her closest friend's deep desire for a husband and a houseful of children. The primary culprit, the central focus of her anger, was the man, whoever he was, who had fathered her.

Her tears continued as she unearthed these secrets, analyzing her long-suppressed emotions and struggling with the new reality of my presence in her life. Though she was welcoming me now and enjoying exploring this new relationship, she could not erase the scars of the past, she said. She still could not look me in the eye and refer to me as "Dad."

"Just saying that word brings me pain," she said.

She tried three times to call her step-father "Dad." The last time she had used the word had been almost ten years before, when she offered him a Father's Day card, only to have him drop it on the counter and respond that he wasn't her father. Not only did he not embrace her as a daughter, she said, but he seemed only to see her as a threat, a competitor for her mother's attention. When he would go away on business trips, she said, it was like paradise. But when he was home, she couldn't even seek comfort in her mom's room when a nightmare scared her. That was the last man she had ever tried to call "Dad," she said.

My heart hurt for her once again. For most kids, I thought, the word brings a sense of comfort and safety. For Heidi, it brought only dread, a feeling of rejection rather than security.

We went on to talk about how hard it was for her to accept and relate to me as "father" because that absentee figure had evoked such negative feelings. She had always concluded her father didn't want anything to do with her. Her thoughts were, if I meant something to him, then why didn't he ever come around?

"Thoughts of your heavenly father probably touched off the same feelings," I told her. "You probably wondered, where is God when I need him? He must not care about me."

When we met," I continued, "you realized your concept of me was wrong. I've always cared about you and have felt the pain of our separation. Likewise, you are wrong in thinking God has not considered you very important to him. The truth is, his care and love for you goes far deeper than mine."

To Heidi, the word "dad" conjured up feelings of worthlessness, insignificance, inferiority. It served only as a grim reminder of the rejection she felt. "I can't change those things, no matter how much of a father I am to you," I told her. "You need something only God can give. In order for you to be free to enjoy calling me 'Dad,' he needs to eliminate the hurt of rejection you've carried all your life."

Heidi was crying softly. I asked if I could pray with her, asking God to remove the anger, bitterness, and sadness that had accumulated over the years. She nodded yes and put her hand in mine. My prayer was that God would free her from the torment of rejection and show her the tangible evidence of his love by enabling her to call me "Dad."

On the afternoon of our third day in Columbia, Heidi and I decided to get a little exercise. Near our neighborhood is a trail that stretches back into the woods. We set off for a jog down the trail. I pulled ahead and put in a good run, while Heidi kept a slower pace behind. When I hit the two-mile mark, I circled back. Soon I met up again with Heidi, and from there we started walking back toward the car. We were both in the mood to have fun, being together.

"Do you remember all those piggyback rides I used to give you when you were a kid," I said, introducing a little sarcasm to our clowning around. She laughed.

"Hop on," I said, bracing myself for her five-foot-eight-inch frame. "Man, you've gotten bigger," I said, as she leaped onto my back.

"Giddy-up, horsey," she said, acting like a kindergartner.

I could only carry her for awhile, so I dropped her off and we started walking together. I was a few yards ahead when she stopped at a wooden bridge.

"Heidi, come on, we gotta go," I said, knowing that supper was waiting. She didn't move. She was gazing over the rail into the stream below. Some thought seemed to have seized her.

She looked up at me, tears moistening her cheeks. Our eyes met for a long moment as she pondered a significant choice. I waited, with no idea what had gripped her mind and stirred her emotions. Suddenly she ran toward me, her arms outstretched.

"I love you, Dad," she said, wrapping her arms around my neck.

14

A DAY IN COURT

Shortly after my first meeting with Heidi, I began talking with Dewey, an attorney in our church, about what legal steps would need to be taken to make our relationship official. I was eager to proceed as quickly as possible with the procedure for declaring me Heidi's father.

My attorney explained that what we needed to do was petition the court for joint custody and, in so doing, establish the fact that I was the biological father. I talked with Holly about this, and she was fully supportive. So we filed our petition.

We scheduled the court date during Heidi's Christmas visit so she and I could appear together. The courtroom was dark; the only lights on were toward the front where the judge was positioned. The walls were a deep mustard color, and the air seemed musty. As we sat down in the back, waiting for our case to come up, I told Heidi how interesting I thought it was to appear before this judge who I just realized had visited our church before and heard me share our story. It both excited Heidi and calmed her anxiety about taking the witness stand. We ended up having to wait through several other cases. We were worried about the delay because Heidi was leaving that afternoon. If the judge didn't get to our case, Heidi wouldn't be able to be there. Finally, our turn came.

"All right. Proceed," the judge said.

"Call Joseph A. Tosini," Dewey said. I walked to the witness stand. It seemed amusing going through the swearing in motions, thinking the judge and I were in somewhat of a role-reversal. Instead of her coming to my sanctuary to hear me give my opinion on matters meaningful to her, I was in her courtroom wanting her opinion on a matter very meaningful to me.

"Do you swear to tell the truth, the whole truth. . ." I noticed a little smile on her face. I think it seemed ironic to her, too.

"Would you please state your name for the record?" Dewey said, after I took my seat.

"Joseph A. Tosini."

"I am going to ask you a few questions regarding Heidi. Are you aware that she was born on January 22nd, 1969, at . . . ." He named the hospital and town in Maryland.

"Yes," I said.

"And are you here stating that you are the biological father of that child?"

"Yes," I said, glancing over at Heidi. I smiled at her. I had to keep myself from making a wise crack about our common noses. After all, these were serious legal issues.

Dewey asked a couple of other questions that were important for the court record. Then he got down to some critical details. "You are coming here today to acknowledge that you are the father of the child, and you have done so publicly before we have come to court here?"

"Yes," I said.

"And you and I have met and discussed this matter, and I have advised you of the ramifications of being legally declared the parent of an individual; is that correct?"

"Yes," I said. Dewey had explained that this petition would immediately give Heidi full rights to my estate—the same rights the others in my immediate family have had. It would also obligate me to provide for Heidi's support, which I had already begun to do.

Dewey went through several more questions to establish that, unlike most custody cases, I was not asking the court for visitation rights, nor was Holly asking for child support. Once that was established, then Dewey gave me the chance I had waited for, to make an official public statement under oath about my view of my reunion with Heidi.

"Is there anything else you wish to add to your petition for declaration of paternity?" Dewey asked.

Looking toward the judge, I said I did, that I wanted to say that God has brought this about. "Before I came to the realization that Jesus was real, alive, and that God was interested in me, Heidi was conceived. . . ."

Now I was beginning to feel less like I was in a staid courtroom and more like I was just in a room talking to people about the realities of life. Everyone in the courtroom seemed to be listening now.

"I had to commit her into his keeping all these years, because I didn't know where she was. And he brought her back, and I am just thrilled." I looked at Heidi, smiling. She smiled in return.

"In fact," I continued, looking back again toward the judge, "this is one of the happiest days of my life, being here in court today." The judge smiled, seeming to appreciate the change of pace from her usual docket of disputes.

"It's unusual for people to be happy in court, Mr. Tosini," she said. Then she asked me a few questions, primarily to be sure I fully understood what these proceedings meant. Afterwards she turned to Dewey and surprised us all.

"There has not been any kind of request for change of name of this child; is that correct?" she asked.

Dewey explained that we had planned to take that step later.

"Okay," she said. "Because sometimes in connection with paternity actions the court does consider that."

I perked up at that comment. It seemed she was willing to take care of the name change then. "If it could be done," I said, glancing toward Dewey and hoping I wasn't speaking out of order, "we'd love to do it."

She asked if Holly would consent, and Dewey assured her that she had already approved the change. Then Dewey officially submitted the request that the name change be part of this petition.

Dewey called Heidi to testify next. Heidi had been nervous about having to answer questions in front of a judge in the cold confines of a courtroom. "You have been present while I was asking the questions to Joseph A. Tosini here today?" Dewey asked.

"Yes," she said.

"And did you hear all the answers?"

"Yes."

"If I were to ask you similar questions, would your answers be the same?" Dewey had come up with a gracious way to save Heidi from having to fill in all the details.

"Yes," she said.

"So you are in agreement with this."

"Yes."

"And I take it from talking with you, you are happy to be here today to have this done."

"Yes," Heidi said, "very much so."

Dewey then asked Heidi if she wanted to proceed with the name change. She said she did and that she and her mother had agreed on the new name.

After tying up the loose ends, the judge made her proclamation: "Upon the evidence, the court finds that all jurisdictional prerequisites have been met and that the petitioner, Joseph A. Tosini, is the natural father. . . . Petitioner's name is ordered changed."[1]

It was official, and I was beaming. I hugged Heidi, who was smiling excitedly also. The judge adjourned the hearing and smiled as she watched us all exchange hugs. Our enthusiasm had seemed to brighten this dark room. Once we were outside, we saw a friend driving by.

"Hey, Clay," Heidi called, enthusiastically. "I'm a Tosini!"

A VISIT EAST

A few weeks after Heidi's holiday visit to Missouri, I made arrangements for another trip to the East Coast, where I would see her once again.

I traveled with another friend, and we had scheduled a work itinerary that included stops in Washington, D.C., Pennsylvania, and New York. I wanted as much time with Heidi as possible, so I worked it out to start the trip in the Washington area, which was near Heidi's home, then bring her along with us for the northern leg of the trip.

After we took care of our business near Washington, D.C., Heidi met us at our motel and the three of us had dinner together. The next day was to be her eighteenth birthday. It so happened that we had a one-day break in our schedule, so before we headed north, we planned a ski trip to a nearby resort.

The next morning, by the time my friend, Bob, and I had arrived from our motel, a fierce winter blizzard had moved in. Enough snow was on the ground that Heidi's school was cancelled, and we had to consider whether to go on with the trip. But Heidi was eager to celebrate her birthday with a ski trip, so we let our adventurous enthusiasm override our common sense.

Bob and I loaded into the car with Holly and Heidi and took off. Though we were barely able to see the road and the forty-minute drive stretched into a nerve-wracking two-hour journey, we made it.

Heidi, an experienced skier, was decked out in her fashionable ski bib, white with blue trim. She spent the day gliding down the mountain with ease. Her knees managed the moguls, her weight shifted just right to carve the turns, and she sped down steep drops where less experienced skiers like me spent most of their time digging out of the powder and trying to strap their skis back on.

She was a little embarrassed to be seen with me from the start. Bob and I hadn't anticipated a ski trip, so all we had to wear were blue jeans and borrowed sweaters. We looked more like we were dressed for a Midwestern hoedown than an Eastern ski slope.

At one point, she was about ready to disown me as her father. Heidi, Bob, and I had approached the ski lift and had to arrange ourselves so two could ride together and one alone. Heidi would go in front, we had decided, with Bob and me following.

"Okay," Bob said, "now where are we supposed to go?"

The people in line ahead of us skied forward just enough to position themselves for the lift. The seat swung around quickly. As it hit the backs of their legs, they settled onto the seats and were lifted off smoothly up the hill. It was Heidi's turn.

"Wait a minute," I said. "How do we do this?"

"Oh, just watch," Heidi said. "Just push with your poles up to where the marker is and bend your knees. Just follow me," Heidi said impatiently, propelling herself to the proper point. Our confusion was irritating her.

The lift swung around swiftly. Heidi slid smoothly into position and waited for the bar to arrive. She sank gracefully onto the lift chair and started up the mountain. Bob and I shuffled forward like an awkward pair of penguins, struggling to walk our skis to meet the lift in time.

"Come on!" I called, trying to uncross my skis.

"Move over!" Bob replied, working to get his skis untangled from mine.

Suddenly, in the midst of our struggle, the bar arrived.

WHAM!

It hit Bob's legs, and he crashed back onto the lift seat. His knees hit the back of my legs and I collapsed onto his lap. As the lift dragged us forward with our ski tips entangled, something went wrong with the machinery.

One of the workers started yelling frantically to another, who scrambled over toward the lift motor and pulled the safety switch, bringing the entire lift to a halt.

There I was hanging in mid-air, trapped on my friend's lap, my skis twisted, my ineptitude displayed before dozens of fashionably attired skiers waiting below us to ascend the slope. All the way up the mountain, faces were turning around to see why the lift had stopped.

Heidi couldn't even look. She was resting her forehead on her hands, shaking her head back and forth in disbelief. I was sure she was secretly hoping no one would realize she knew us.

By this time we were laughing so hard we could barely get ourselves untangled. No one else seemed to think it was funny, though. Including Heidi. We were cutting into their skiing time.

"Yeah, we really own the slopes," I said to Bob, gasping for air amid the laughter.

We tried after that to be more careful boarding the lifts. But the adventure continued as we tried to navigate the mogul runs and explore new trails. No matter how hard I tried, I couldn't keep up with Heidi.

The day was such pure fun, it was hard to see it come to an end. In fact, once we got home, got warm, and into dry clothes, Heidi suggested to her mom that we just stay there since they had plenty of extra room in the house.

Holly agreed, and worked out the sleeping arrangements. To make room for us, Heidi would sleep with her mom, and I would sleep in Heidi's room. Bob would stay in the guest room. We were worn out from our skiing expedition, so sleep came easily.

Early the next morning, just about dawn, the door opened softly and Heidi stood there looking at me. Very quietly, she crossed the room and gingerly crawled into the bed to curl up alongside me.

Immediately I thought of the countless nights my other girls had come into my room during the night—maybe because of a nightmare, because of hearing noises, or maybe just because they wanted to be close to me. But here was a young lady who had never had the privilege as a little girl to snuggle next to her daddy, one who was forced to endure her nightmares and night noises without the comfort of a father's arms.

Once again, despite the good time we'd had on the slopes that day, the pain of the missing years returned. How badly little girls need their fathers, I thought. How could I ever make up for the lost time?

Emotions overwhelmed me as I turned toward Heidi and saw she was crying. I pulled her close to me and let my tears flow as well. In that moment, I instinctively knew how she felt and what she was trying to tell me. Somehow she wanted to communicate how much she had missed me and how happy she was we were finally together. With this expression of trust, she was making herself vulnerable to me as her father.

As we lay there without talking, the barriers melted between us. I understood more completely why I had such a strong desire to embrace her, to hold her hand, to be physically close, and I knew it was a good thing. It was the same inclination I felt when my other children were born, an inclination to hold them, to cuddle them, to communicate to them that I was with them, that I loved them, that I would protect them. It was sad to think that affection was so often understood solely as a means of physical pleasure. Affection is a confirmation of acceptance necessary for emotional security. I knew Heidi's old foundations of mistrust and abandonment were being replaced with a proper understanding of a father's love. I couldn't help wondering how many children were being defiled as they reached out to the person they instinctively wanted most to trust.

Afterward, I told Holly about Heidi coming into the room. She was also deeply moved by Heidi's actions. She had heard her crawl out of her bed and intuitively knew she was seeking out her father's acceptance and protection. It touched Holly to see Heidi reaching out to me like that.

Later that day we took off for my parents' home in New York. On our way, I thought about how grateful I was for the open-heartedness with which they had received Heidi—the grandchild they had known nothing about.

After the initial reunion with Heidi, I had called and said I wanted to fly to New York for a few days, and that I had something important to talk to them about. They didn't know what to expect.

"Do you remember when your front doorbell rang when I was here last month?" I asked.

"Yes, you said it was someone who knew an old friend of yours," my mother said. "What about it?"

"Well, that man at the door came to tell me that I had a seventeen-year-old daughter."

"What?" she said. I explained what happened in California years before.

"Are you sure she's your child?" my father asked. I put Heidi's picture in front of them.

"Oh my God," my mother said, putting her head down on the table. The resemblance was undeniable. After we talked more about the past, my father asked how Jodi and Joy had responded and why I had waited so long to tell them. I told him I hadn't wanted to burden my mother and him with something they could do nothing about.

After the shock subsided, my father spoke. "This is good news," he said. Then, turning toward my mother, he said, "Congratulations! We've got another granddaughter."

He walked over and gave me a big hug. A sense of relief came over me. My father didn't make a habit of pointing his finger at people, highlighting their mistakes. He was more prone to forgive than to judge.

"I'm happy for you," he said.

My mother and father had flown to Columbia to be with us the weekend of Heidi's first visit, and they also had seen her at Christmas. But other than those rather crowded get-togethers, this was their first opportunity to spend some unhurried hours alone with her. When Heidi, Bob, and I arrived in New York, we got settled at my parents' house and began sorting out our plans.

I had been invited to speak on Friday night at a church in one of the roughest sections of the Bronx. My parents were eager to have some time with Heidi, and they made it clear that they didn't feel the

Bronx was the best place for her to be on a Friday night.

"You stay here with us, Heidi," my mother said. "With a father like yours," she added with a touch of humor, "you'll have plenty of chances to visit churches." Heidi was as eager to stay as they were to have her.

Later that night, after everyone else had gone to bed, I stayed up talking with Heidi. We were sitting on the couch with my arm around her.

"How was your first evening alone with your grandparents?" I asked. She said she had really enjoyed them. My parents were lavishing attention on Heidi, giving her special gifts, treating her with the affection they had shown their other grandchildren since birth.

That night, they had had dinner together and had gone out to a movie. They had told her a little about me, she said, recounting some of their memories of me growing up in Brooklyn. They had walked her through the living room, pointing out portraits and snapshots of Jodi and Joy and other family members. Each photograph carried a story with it, part of a string of wonderful memories of their grandchildren.

"They've been living here all my life," she said, sadly, "and I never knew."

Up until now, I realized she had only been wrestling with the years she had lost out on knowing me. Now she realized she had missed out on knowing a great set of grandparents as well. She wasn't there for the Thanksgivings, Christmases, and birthdays with these grandparents, who had invested so much in their other grandchildren. Jodi and Joy's pictures were all over the walls, the endtables, and the mantel, but her picture was nowhere to be found. Her face didn't appear in these grandparents' special memories. She turned away suddenly.

"I hate you," she said, with tears welling up. "I hate you. . . . I hate you. . . ."

The words stung. I knew that the fires of resentment toward me had burned inside her over the years. What I didn't know was how and when her resentment would emerge—and whether we would be able to get beyond it.

"Why didn't you come get me?" she went on. In my mind, I

pictured a child trapped in a room, screaming for someone to come open the door. "You weren't there when I needed you. And I'll never be able to bring back those years."

This was the flood of emotion I had dreaded the most. I knew that none of my explanations would erase her pain. Nothing I could say would justify my choices that had ended up causing her to suffer. Yet I knew we had to walk through this terrain, as tough as it would be. Carefully, I took the first steps.

"We can't bring back the past," I said. "I wish I could change things. But I can't." She was still looking away, but she was allowing me to hold her hand.

"In a relationship," I said, "the only way someone who's innocent and someone who's guilty can get together is when the innocent one forgives. I'm guilty," I said, not trying to explain away the decisions I had made. "I need for you to forgive me."

Lifting her hand to her cheek, she wiped away her tears. "I don't want to need you," she said, fighting through her own feelings. I could tell she was immersed in a confusing array of powerful emotions, and I couldn't tell which way things would turn. We sat quietly for a few moments, with me pondering what to say next. I wanted to be sure she understood that I had not been breezing through life all these years, unburdened by the pain she had known. I didn't want her to feel sorry for me; but I wanted her to know that I always had cared deeply about her.

"You're the one who was ripped off," I said. "It would be easy for you to be angry because you're innocent. But being guilty doesn't lessen the hurt, the frustration, the disappointment." She was listening intently.

Regret would always be there, I said. We would not be able to reclaim the years, rewrite the script so that she could have enjoyed a father during her childhood. But we don't have to cling to the anger, the bitterness, or the hate. Forgiveness can take that away. And once forgiveness does its work, then only regret remains. And, I added, no one slides through life without ending up with many regrets.

Though she was confronting her pain and anger, I wanted this encounter to be an opportunity for her to understand more about life.

I wanted her to understand that life is more than just a set of random circumstances. "God has a purpose for your life," I told her. "Your tragedy could be a good teacher. More lessons come through heartbreak than through heart throbs. It may be," I continued, "that the pain we have both experienced could somehow help us better understand what life is about."

Into my mind flashed the image of a woman in the Bible who learned something about mercy. "There's a story in the Bible about a woman who was caught sinning," I said. "The religious leaders brought her to Jesus and wanted him to say it was okay to kill her for what she had done. But Jesus confounded their plan," I told her. "He said, 'Let the person who has no sin throw the first stone.' After shifting their attention from the woman to themselves, they each began to drop their stones and walk away, beginning with the oldest."

"The older you get," I told Heidi, "the more you realize how weak you are."

I went on with the story. "Only Jesus and the woman were left. Her accusers were all gone. Jesus was the only one who had the right to throw a stone, but he forgave the woman instead. 'Neither do I condemn you,' he said."

"Heidi, you're seventeen years old," I continued, "and I've only known you for a couple of months. But I'm well aware that you have some embarrassing things in your life, things that you've done that were wrong. You're going to do a lot more things that are wrong, too."

I put my hand under her chin and turned her face toward me. I wanted her to see my eyes. "Heidi, I forgive you," I said. "Now I have no right, nor am I demanding you to forgive me, but . . ." I said, crying myself by this time.

She looked at me, her eyes softer. I could tell from her face she loved me and that she wanted to forgive me. A door seemed to open in her heart. She reached her arms out and hugged me.

"I love you, Heidi," I said, my mind racing with questions about what this teenager was feeling.

We sat together for a few more minutes. She didn't say much. But

I could tell that rather than slamming the door in my face, she had left it ajar. The door to restoration was open. By this time, it was near 3 a.m., so we said goodnight and headed for our bedrooms.

Stretched out in bed, I lay awake pondering the joy and sadness once again mingling in my heart. Despite the anguish, it was satisfying to communicate as father to daughter on such a deep level. Many parents and children never make this kind of contact, I thought, even if they live in the same house for twenty years. But sadness came when I thought about Heidi looking through all her grandparents' pictures, thinking to herself that if life had been fair, hers could have been there, too. Finally I closed my eyes, thanking the Lord for His mercy, for the hope He had given me for our relationship. Just before falling asleep, I slipped in one final prayer:

"Thank you, Lord, for parents who love me more than I deserve. . . . Help me deal with Heidi the same way they've dealt with me."

*F*AMILY MATTERS

In order to move toward the destination I was determined to reach and to find answers to the many questions that lined the path, it seemed clear that Heidi should come live with us in Missouri for a time. She had flown out from Maryland four times in our first six months together to get acquainted with Dawn, Jodi, and Joy. But I wanted her relationships to go beyond the formal status of a temporary houseguest to the point where she could just become part of the family. This step, of course, would plunge us into unknown territory; we didn't know what might happen or what complications could emerge. Our relationships had fared well on a long-distance basis, but we hadn't exposed them to the daily push-and-pull of family life with its strains, stress, and conflict. Everything could explode in our faces; there were no guarantees.

I couldn't promise Heidi a picnic—only regular life. "I don't want you to be Queen For A Day," I told her, "I just want you to be a normal sister in a normal family. I want you to be able to get mad at me, and I want to feel free to get mad at you. We'll laugh. We'll cry. You'll tease people, and you'll get teased. And we'll all get frustrated at times." But I assured her that experiences such as these are the mortar which cements relationships.

Heidi was making plans after her high school graduation to attend a prestigious art school in Philadelphia. An art teacher who had befriended Heidi and nurtured her talents for four years encouraged her to pursue art as a career. The teacher identified this college as the prime place for Heidi to refine her talents, and she wrote her a strong recommendation. When Heidi became the second student from the teacher's class ever to be accepted into the program—with a scholarship offer to top it off—they were both ecstatic. Heidi's heart was set on going, and after we toured the campus together and spoke to the dean, I paid a non-refundable deposit guaranteeing her place in the fall class.

My proposal to have Heidi come live in Missouri for a year, though, meant postponing art school in Philadelphia. Heidi's teacher thought this would be a big mistake. "You might never have the opportunity for this type of education again," she told her. "Think of yourself and your future. You can go places."

As Heidi labored over her college plans, she fought through other worries as well. I let her know that she would be free to be herself, free to think and explore. She was concerned about being thrust into the "church" community of which I was a part, and I assured her that I wouldn't cram an assortment of religious formulas down her throat. She was also concerned about being thrust into the middle of a new family, larger than the one-child household to which she was accustomed. And this family had another brand new arrival as well: a newborn boy, Joseph.

Heidi's mom left the responsibility for making the decision to Heidi. But many others were offering her their opinions, warning of the potential hazards.

"You've been an only child and grown up with a certain way of doing things. You're set in your ways; they're set in theirs. . . ."

"With two younger sisters and a baby, it will be hard on the family. You'll just be in the way. . . ."

"Don't be stupid and blow your career. You can go visit your family on holidays. . . ."

The decision was made more difficult because the counsel she was receiving was coming from people she respected, people she knew were concerned about her welfare and were trying to shield her from harm. She didn't want to disregard what they were saying or let them down.

People close to me were also questioning the wisdom of bringing

Heidi to Columbia at what seemed an inopportune time. "With a new baby, don't you need to be considerate of your household? Do you really think you should impose this girl on your family?"

It was a risk, and risks are never easy. The safest bet was to have Heidi launch out on her own and avoid the trauma of trying to merge separate worlds, conflicting lifestyles, diverse personalities. But in this case, I wasn't trying to play things conservatively—exchange some letters and phone calls and have Heidi come for Christmas—and settle for a minimal relationship. Even though Heidi hadn't known us for eighteen years, she was as much a part of our family as our new son. We accepted him without regard for the "inconvenience" a baby would cause. Likewise, I wanted Heidi to be embraced by our family and feel as much a daughter and sister in our family as Jodi and Joy. And I honestly believed that was the right thing to do.

When Heidi and I talked on the phone one night, I offered what I thought was the best reason for her coming: "When you're older," I said, "having a friendship with your sisters may be more significant than spending an extra year in college." Heidi was open to what I was saying and, to me, that spoke highly of her values and her ability to discern what was important. My optimism that night was confirmed several months later when Heidi decided to come.

Once the course was set, I knew the questions that had been suppressed for the first months of our reunion would be explored. The initial euphoria would give way to the more threatening realities of the relational adjustments that this change required. It didn't take long before we were tackling the issue we hadn't yet been forced to confront: Who's the boss?

The incident that triggered the showdown was my intrusion into Heidi's social life. I told her that when she came to live with us the first several months would be a major adjustment requiring all the emotional strength she could muster. I didn't think it would be wise to add any additional pressure, namely boys. Not long after Heidi got settled into our house, my fatherly authority was challenged. She mentioned a young man who showed an interest in spending some time with her. I felt strongly that type of distraction would be an overload on her emotional capacities.

Before leaving on a trip for Europe, I mentioned my concern to the boy's father. He understood my reasons and agreed it would be best for Heidi to concentrate on adjusting to her new family. When I returned ten days later, Heidi was clearly not overjoyed to see me. In fact, she didn't speak to me for several days. Finally, when I got the opportunity, I made the effort to end the cold war. I walked into her room and sat down on her bed.

"What's the matter?" I asked.

In a moment, the answer came out in a storm of anger. "What do you think you're doing, trying to run my life from six thousand miles away?" She obviously resented what she perceived to be my controlling her life.

So far, since our reunion, Heidi had not experienced this less pleasant side of having a father. We'd had fun. We'd talked. We'd hugged. Now, we were fighting. As any father or mother knows, that's part of the parenting package.

"I didn't come into your life just to be your friend," I told her as gently as I could, sitting on the side of her bed. "We're not just pretending that I'm your dad, you know." I tried to read her reaction. It worried me some to be tangling so soon after her Missouri move, just as she was getting settled. But I knew something like this would have to happen sooner or later.

"Fathers have a tendency to want to influence their children's lives," I explained, still hoping to ease some of the tension between us. "As your father, I have authority in your life, and I intend to exercise it. You've had some of the joys, now you're going to have some of the headaches." This kind of input from a father was so new to her that I don't think she knew how to react. She sat quietly, pondering my words.

"My responsibility is to do what I think is best for you. I'm trying to protect you," I concluded, offering the ultimate reason for what seemed to her as unwelcome interference in her choices.

She had started crying. By now I figured she was not going to fight me. In fact, I suspected that it felt good to her not to be facing life's choices alone.

"Heidi, I make mistakes, but I do love you," I told her. "And I'm going to do the best I can to be what I think a father is supposed to be. That's not just a provider and protector, but at times that means giving the final word as well." I reached my arms toward her, and she lifted her face and drew her arms around me.

I assumed Heidi had spoken to her mother about this situation, and I was curious what Holly's reaction would be.

"Did you talk to your mother about this?" I asked.

"Yes," she replied.

"What did you tell her?"

"I said, 'Who does he think he is?'" Heidi said.

"And what did she say?"

She hesitated a bit. And then a tiny smile crept onto her tear-moistened cheeks. "She said, 'Maybe he thinks he's your father.'"

During the first year of our reunion, Heidi's closest contact had been with me. She was confident of my acceptance, but Heidi was cautious at first with Dawn, not knowing quite how to respond to her. She felt awkward in their times alone together. Heidi was unsure how much she was wanted, uncertain of how far Dawn's acceptance of her would go. She was fearful that she might ignore her, treating her like a prop on the scene, or worse, as a threat to her and her family.

Before Heidi arrived, Dawn had the idea to let Heidi decorate her own room rather than having everything done for her. So as soon as Heidi came, she and Dawn took on the task of converting what had been our guest room into Heidi's bedroom. The project required hours of planning and searching through wallpaper books and paint color charts. It gave them a chance to interact alone without having to constantly deal directly with the initial awkwardness of their relationship. Over the weeks, I observed a camaraderie developing. It didn't take long for Heidi to perceive Dawn's sincerity.

In addition to the redecorating project, Dawn made it a point during those early weeks to incorporate Heidi into the daily household chores. Dawn set up a rotation for Jodi, Joy, and Heidi that included washing dishes, making dinner, preparing the salad, and cleaning the table. As Dawn worked with Heidi to help her learn practical details of our household, like cooking and caring for the baby, Heidi seemed to look to Dawn with more and more respect. Dawn did everything she could to make Heidi feel a full member of the family, with both the privileges and the responsibilities. I could tell that after several months, Heidi had become fully confident that Dawn truly accepted and loved her.

Dawn found great satisfaction in her relationship with Heidi. For so many years Dawn had carried with me the burden of this young girl we didn't know. Now she was having the opportunity to help nurture her and prepare her in very practical ways for her future. Dawn's investment, too, seemed to help make up for the lost years.

Heidi showed the extent to which Dawn had proven her commitment to her when on a church women's retreat, a leader asked the women to write on a slip of paper the name of their closest friend. The question made Heidi consider what a close friend was to her: someone with whom she felt free to talk on a deep level, someone who wanted to listen, someone with whom she could share confidences. When she thought about someone who fit that description, she was rather surprised with her answer. She wrote down the name "Dawn."

About five months after Heidi had moved into our home, I had an aggravating interaction with a visiting pastor's wife who had recently learned of my reunion with Heidi. "She's living in your home!" she said, showing her shock, along with an undertone of disapproval. "How could your wife handle that since she isn't even her own child?" To me, her tone of voice almost indicated that Dawn and Jodi and Joy must not have any self-respect to allow in an "outsider," especially one born under circumstances less dignified than theirs. This is a preacher's wife, I thought to myself, the kind who goes around saying she believes in miracles, the kind who talks about humility and forgiveness, and yet she didn't seem to have much hope for love to triumph in a relationship.

As I glanced at her puzzled face, I thought about how critical Dawn's commitment and support was to the healing that Heidi was undergoing. I thought about the investment Dawn was making in the life of an eighteen-year-old girl just preparing to face an adult world.

I offered the woman the fullest explanation I could think of as to why Dawn would want to embrace a situation like this:

"She's a Christian," I said, looking her in the eye. "A real one."

In the beginning I directed much of my attention and effort toward Heidi. I was trying hard—maybe too hard—to make her secure, constantly evaluating whether she was struggling, constantly trying to ease her adjustment process. At the time, I didn't see fully the impact this focused attention had on Dawn, Jodi, and Joy. Too often I would leave them to draw on an emotional savings account I assumed was there from the years we had been together. Though they valiantly opened their hearts to incorporate Heidi into our family life, they grew frustrated with my inattention to their needs and feelings.

One night, this hurt my daughter Joy. I had slipped downstairs to say goodnight to Joy and Heidi, who were sleeping together that night in Heidi's room. Joy was lying still. Assuming she was asleep, I began talking quietly to Heidi: "I'm glad you're here, Heidi. I'm really glad you're my daughter," I said. "I love you dearly." I bent over and gave her a big hug and kiss.

Then I noticed Joy move. "Oh, are you awake, Joy?" I asked. No answer. Without a word, she turned toward the wall, yanking the covers up to where they nearly covered her head. I leaned over to her and said, "Is everything okay?" Silence.

Suddenly I realized what had happened. She had listened to my gentle words to Heidi and was stung by my seemingly exclusive affection toward her. Joy must have begun wondering whether I had the same feelings toward her. After all, she had shown a great willingness to share her father with her new sister, but she hadn't bargained for losing me altogether.

Joy was a *joy* to me; I couldn't love her any more. It hurt for me to think that she would somehow assume she had lost ground with me or that my affection for her had diminished because of Heidi's arrival. When Joseph first came, the girls didn't feel any less loved because I was caught up in enjoying him. Now I was giving Heidi the same affection I was giving a new baby. She was the new arrival who needed to be acclimated into the household.

What could I do, I wondered. I believed I had to continue trying to penetrate Heidi's skepticism, proving to her that, for the first time, she had a father in her life who cared for her, a father she could trust. But it hurt to see the rest of my family feeling cut off from my affections. I felt pulled apart.

It hurt Dawn to see the obvious imbalance of my attention during that period. While she was pouring out her love to Heidi, she also worried about Jodi and Joy, who were having to step aside for a time and allow someone else to take center stage in my life, someone who hadn't even been on the stage before. They were both at a crucial age in life, the beginning of adolescence. But crises don't come at convenient times. Babies don't wait for their parents to awaken from a peaceful sleep before they start screaming; cars get stuck in snow, not in sunshine.

My only hope was that God would cover my shortcomings and protect my family from any seeds of resentment that could take root and tear apart what I believed he was trying to bring together.

"Help us hang on," I prayed, "through the turbulence."

One concern of mine was that our decision to have Heidi come live with us would be evaluated by the daily "temperature" of our household. It was a temptation to observe a conflict—for example, Dawn becoming upset when Heidi came home late for dinner—as an indicator that something was critically wrong or that Heidi's coming was a mistake. Strife emerges in every household, and I didn't want our family to have to live up to a standard to which we could never attain. Nobody gives up in a normal home when two sisters have an argument over who's going to clear the table. Families don't throw in the towel because it has been a lousy week.

And certainly we did have weeks like that. One reoccurring complaint was that our thirteen- and fourteen-year-olds didn't have as many freedoms or as much fun as their eighteen-year-old sister.

"Do we have to go to bed now? Heidi's not."

"Why can't we go to the concert in St. Louis, Dad? Heidi is."

"Heidi can drink coffee. Why can't I?" The younger girls felt like they were getting shortchanged; Heidi felt like they were trying to drag her back into junior high. And Dawn and I had to field their frustrations.

Heidi had suddenly exchanged the serenity of her Maryland home for a household bustling with three teenagers and a continual parade of overnight guests, visiting family members, and friends. It left her feeling like she was fighting for her privacy—and often losing.

One night she was by herself downstairs, quietly curled up in a chair, writing some letters. She was concentrating under the glow of a small lamp when suddenly her dim solitude was flooded with light, while the loud thumps descending the stairway announced sister Jodi had arrived. She passed by singing a tune, and without a word headed straight for the VCR—with an exercise video in hand. Next, the crackle of television static filled the room. Jodi worked the controls, then, waiting for the tape to rewind, flipped on the radio.

Heidi's temperature was climbing steadily. Not even the courtesy of an "excuse me," she thought.

"Would you *mind* turning down the radio," Heidi said with irritation.

"If you don't like it," Jodi returned, "go upstairs." It's something of a miracle that violence didn't break out in our house that night.

All of us were having to make adjustments. Heidi, growing up as an only child, was not accustomed to sharing her space or her possessions. The girls began swapping clothes, but they didn't always follow the same rules. Heidi's clothes closet was one sanctuary she preferred not to have invaded. Yet it became the target of a few sneak attacks from younger sisters scrounging for a blouse or a pair of shoes to wear. Heidi didn't mind loaning her clothes, as long as someone asked her permission. But she became quite unhappy when clothes were taken out of her room unannounced—especially when returned on the floor in a wrinkled heap.

Heidi's bedroom was her private quarters, a place where she could listen to her music and retreat from the more public parts of the household. At one point, she borrowed a music video from a friend for a few days and left it in her room. She left the house, and when she returned, her videotape was playing in the family room. Someone had violated her private space, and she was fuming.

That evening, she was obviously angry but nobody knew why. Heidi was indulging in a pout. Growing up, she had usually kept her emotions inside, waiting for time to cool them off. That seemed to work when she was alone, but in the close quarters of a six-member family, unresolved anger affected everyone. So we had told her: "If something is bugging you, get it out."

That evening, when Dawn and I were together, we asked Heidi what was wrong. She explained her frustration about the video. Dawn said she had turned it on.

"That was mine," Heidi said, "and you just grabbed it?"

"What's wrong with that?" Dawn said. "It was just sitting there." As feelings were aired, the issue soon grew beyond the video . . . beyond her room . . . beyond her privacy. It became Heidi's frustration over the fact that the rest of the family felt comfortable using her clothes and borrowing her things, but she didn't feel free to reciprocate. Although we had given her the free run of the house, she didn't feel comfortable going into the other girl's rooms or digging in the refrigerator for whatever she wanted. Habits we didn't think twice about were very awkward for her. She just wanted us to appreciate how difficult the transition into a new household was for her. And, indeed, it was.

From the onset of our reunion, Heidi and I had talked many times about life, about questions we both had, about a purpose for living, about God. Her mind was active, exploring and testing ideas. I was careful to give her space to think through the questions and confusion of a young mind.

When she was considering the Missouri move, she had asked how it would work to live together since I was a pastor, immersed in a closeknit community of church families and friends, and she wasn't sure what she believed. With the firmness of a young feminist just learning to think for herself, she vowed that she wouldn't conform to the new group that would be surrounding her. She didn't want to lose her identity or her objectivity. She told me of experiences with Christians early in life that had spooked her and prevented her from taking the Bible seriously. She had run into some people who were making a big deal out of monsters coming out of the sea in years to come and secret codes that would be supernaturally emblazoned on people's foreheads. None of that made a bit of sense to her, so she had discounted Christianity as a legitimate way of life.

I couldn't much blame her for the conclusions she had drawn, based on the exposure she had had over the years to people's sometimes silly efforts to make sense of the Bible. I wanted her to have the opportunity to be exposed to a clear Christian message— without having it foisted upon her. After she settled into our house, she did begin coming to the services, though we never forced her. In the beginning, she sat detached, coldly observing the goings-on. After a few months, I noticed her face began looking more pensive.

She began to be more receptive. As I prayed for her during those times, I felt confident God would make himself real to her. Over the next few weeks, I noticed she was more contemplative during the services. Something was stirring inside her. At times she would even go to the front of the church when we would invite people to come forward to pray.

She was struggling with the implications of a decision to yield to this God of which she was becoming more aware. How would it affect the people she knew back in Maryland? A close friend and classmate had told her about a relative who was a born-again Christian; he was "looney tunes," she had said. Heidi also wondered how her mother would respond. Would she be hurt? Would she feel Heidi was turning her back on the way she was raised?

One night, about a year after she moved to Missouri, the obstacles her questions presented had been overcome. She reached the point in her own spiritual journey where she concluded that, contrary to what she first thought, these people she was observing were experiencing something genuine. What she had been seeing and hearing made sense. As she sat in her seat, praying intently about private matters, something new came alive inside.

Many people had questioned the wisdom of bringing Heidi into our household. And sometimes the tension did reach a near breaking point. But rather than anyone breaking, we saw over time that our relationships were growing stronger.

Jodi and Joy, like they always had with each other, were arguing and joking with Heidi over who would wash dishes, and nobody gave it a second thought. Heidi began to get irritated with Dawn, just as Jodi and Joy always had, for expecting her to do so much around the house. It didn't phase anybody. Heidi had simply become one of the family.

Young Joseph was born in March 1987, just before Heidi came to live with us. So, of course, by the time he was able to walk and talk, he knew nothing of the lost years. He had no experience like Jodi, when she found out one day she wasn't my oldest daughter after all. He had no experience like Dawn, who was faced with the major adjustment of incorporating a new person into her household.

One day, it was Joseph who marked the full incorporation of Heidi into our family.

"What's your name?" I asked.

"Joseph," he said, proud to be able to answer his dad's question.

"Do you have a sister?"

"Yes."

"How many sisters do you have?"

"Three."

"What are their names?"

"Joy, Jodi, and . . . ." he said without a moment's hesitation . . . . "Heidi."

For him, it was as if the seventeen-year gap had never happened. For Heidi and me, it was fading further and further into the past.

*F*ATHER'S DAY REVISITED

More than three years have passed since Heidi and I met, and our story continues. Heidi has been attending the University of Missouri in Columbia, where she continues to pursue her talents in art. She now chases Joseph around the neighborhood and gives him rides on the back of our family's mountain bike.

Jodi and Joy are growing into young ladies, and they and Heidi still tease each other, worry about each other, get mad at each other, just like any sisters who have grown up together. Jodi, on her fourth attempt, just got her driver's license. Heidi has her opinions on Jodi's driving ability; Jodi has her opinions on Heidi's opinions.

Some of the tensions have subsided in our family. Dinner conversations are not punctuated with "ice breakers." We don't act like we must walk on eggshells, and neither does Heidi. She feels free to ask for gas money, and I feel free to remind her that they accept her money at the station, too. Now we're able to talk about things we previously were unable to—even joke about them: "Yeah, Heidi," one of the kids will crack, "I remember what a little brat you were as a kid. . . . oh, that's right. I guess I must have been thinking of somebody else."

The awkwardness of the new relationships have worn off, and now we're just left with the joys and struggles every family experiences. Life together has become so routine, in fact, that even while working on this manuscript, Heidi and I had to remind ourselves of what a miracle it was that we are together. It's reminiscent of when

God sent manna in the wilderness to feed the people of Israel. After awhile, the miracle of food dropping out of the sky became almost commonplace; it was not as exciting as garden vegetables: the garlics, leeks, and onions of Egypt. Likewise, we sometimes lose perspective on our miracle, like when Heidi's college tuition bill arrived in the mail. "Ouch," I winced. "This is expensive." But then, I thought, it's also a privilege that I have a daughter to send to college.

I waited to write this book until we got to the point where I knew that Heidi and I were inseparable. We have undergone a restoration, a melding of hearts and lives that cannot be undone. That's not to say that she won't move away. She'll probably get married and have her own life to live. But she will have two sisters and a brother she'll always relate with, along with several nephews and nieces. Her children will have aunts and uncles, cousins, and grandparents that they otherwise wouldn't. And she'll always be our daughter, always be at home with us, regardless of where she lives.

Of course, relationship comes without warranty. Heidi and I could have a falling out. But now it would be no different from any other child who has a falling out with a parent—except, perhaps, that we would have a greater appreciation for the relationship we have had and the realization of what we would lose by forsaking it.

It's at times like this past Father's Day that I'm reminded of the mercy and kindness God has shown us. I marvel when I consider that airplane flight when Heidi shared how difficult it was for her to call me "Dad," and how God answered our prayer on that nature trail. And it wasn't just that she *called* me "Dad." I really became her dad.

Twelve years ago, Heidi offered a man a Father's Day card, hoping he would fill the empty place in her heart where a father belonged. That day Heidi determined she wouldn't give any more Father's Day cards. But two and a half years after our reunion, Heidi noticed the approach of another Father's Day. That day, at age twenty, she handed me a card. The message written in her flowing, artistic handwriting, on a cream colored card that she had bordered with dozens of hearts, proved to me that the secret place in her heart, the place reserved for me, had stopped aching:

Dad,

Happy Father's Day! I want you to know that I love you very much, and even at times when it doesn't show, deep down I care. It's hard for me to express my love to you in a few short words. . . . I'm so thankful Jesus kept us safe for so many years and then brought us together to be one!

I love you, Daddy!
Heidi

SECTION THREE:

HOPE FOR A WOUNDED WORLD

*R*AW REALITIES

As I've shared this story of Heidi with people over these last years, I've been surprised at their responses. Quite often, I'll be with a stranger, perhaps someone seated next to me on an airplane, exchanging everyday chit-chat: where we've been, what we do for a living, how a certain airline or baseball club ought to be run. The conversation generally stays on a fairly surface level; neither of us is venturing into any vulnerable territory. Sometimes the course of conversation leads me to mention that my college-age daughter and I first met just a few years ago. Some people register shock. Some feel embarrassed for me. Some act like this isn't something we should be talking about. But I usually smile and make some comment like, "Oh no, I don't mind. Our story has a happy ending."

As I go on to tell about the years without Heidi and the heartache I felt, the protective fences around people begin to come down. Many open up and tell of sorrows life has brought them and of relational wounds they continue to bear. Men have similar accounts of how they fathered a child they never knew and how it has haunted them. Some women describe the pain of a father's rejection or the physical or sexual abuse they suffered as a child.

As I've talked and sometimes cried with people who have reacted strongly to my story, I have come to better comprehend the extent to which we live in a wounded world. Whatever the circumstances responsible for our wounds, however deep in the past they might be buried, all of us must reckon with their lasting impact.

Though my story began with heartache, my reunion with Heidi started a thrilling chapter for me. But it took time to unfold; I knew I couldn't rush things. Several months after meeting Heidi a television producer who had heard our saga had tried to set up an interview. But I knew it was not yet time. Only after I knew Heidi trusted me and was secure in my love for her was I confident this was a genuine story of restoration. Only then did I feel comfortable writing down our story and talking to the producer about an interview.

But even now I have the sense that this script is yet unfinished.

Yes, Heidi and I now relate together in a healthy way as father and daughter. I can be happy for Heidi, happy for me—but what about you? What if your story hasn't yet come to a happy conclusion?

I think back to the parents I was with the day their kindergartner was run over by a school bus. Nothing can erase the profound sense of loss those people felt, nor the heartache of that driver. Years later, when one of them sees a yellow bus pull up, and a small boy clutching a lunch box bounces down the steps, the ache will be felt afresh. The loss will be as real and meaningful in thirty years as it was on that fateful day.

If you, like these parents, face ongoing pain either from the blows you've received, or from the blows you've delivered, I've included this final section aimed at helping open a new chapter in another story—yours.

I am a different person today than I was before Heidi was born. When I pursued the countercultural dream of the late 1960s, my youthful zeal for life threw me into a reckless pursuit of pleasure and self-satisfaction. I didn't set out to hurt anyone; I was just doing basically whatever I felt like. But the dissonance kept getting louder. I came to learn that my choices had consequences and that, even when I regretted the decisions I'd made, I couldn't change the outcome.

To a great extent, the sorrow produced in my life was responsible for knocking me off the road on which I was traveling and re-directing my steps. It forced me to ponder the deeper issues of life, to think about what I was doing, what my life was producing. It was suffering that brought a deeper understanding of what my life was all about.

A friend of mine once related a sobering experience from the Vietnam War. Jimmy was out in the field one morning having a breakfast of C-rations with a few men in his unit. One of the group, a quiet nineteen-year-old kid, began talking about the girl who was waiting for him back home. He pulled out a snapshot from his wallet and passed it around. He was standing beside her, with his arm around her shoulder. The best thing about going home, he said, was that they were going to get married.

A few hours later the unit was fired upon in the jungle, and a gun burst ended this teenager's dreams. The task fell to Jimmy to crawl to him on his belly and attach a grappling hook to the body so it could be dragged away. The last Jimmy saw of him was a body bag thrown into an armored personnel carrier for the journey home. The experience rocked Jimmy to the core. He, too, was nineteen, and he would never be the same.

Exposure to the raw realities of human existence affects us. Suffering forces us to ask why. "What's the point of all this?" "What is life about?" "Is tragedy mere chance or is there something behind it that gives it meaning?" Jimmy said his friend's death brought a depth to his own life that was lacking before.

Another man who was touched by the anguish of life was Solomon, a Hebrew king whom the Bible describes as the wisest man who ever lived. Where did he learn this wisdom? Pain was one of his primers. Life's meaning, Solomon wrote, is better understood in a house of mourning than in the house where there is feasting and laughter. In modern language, we could say people get a much better grasp of what is significant in an intensive care unit than in an amusement park.

Some people do seem to have the capacity to cruise through life unscathed. They smile, laugh, and envelop themselves with enjoyment, somehow avoiding a confrontation with the tough issues of their existence. They can maintain a thin retaining wall between themselves and life's disturbing realities, never having to contemplate a universe that doesn't seem to make sense.

But those confronted by the adversity of life cannot remain insulated. Pain propels them on a journey into deeper questions of meaning where they can consider the truth about the world and the truth about themselves. Pain strips away the protective veneer and exposes the inner self to questions each of us needs to grapple with, because the result of this heart search determines our direction and ultimate destination.

I can offer no simple answers or concise formulas to rid your life of anguish. Instead, I pose a question, "What's more important—to understand the meaning of life or to avoid pain?" Perhaps our goal should not be to eliminate pain but instead to face it and allow it to direct our attention to the deeper issues of life.

The remainder of this book is devoted to the discussion of these issues, and I invite you to explore them with me.

19

THE DEEPER QUESTIONS

As a small child, I remember trembling at the sound of thunder, scampering into my parents' room, and slipping into their bed. The most secure feeling I ever had as a boy was in the midst of those thunderstorms, when my father held me close, my hand in his.

I described earlier the scene just before daybreak when Heidi first crawled in next to me. As we lay there, I remembered how protected I felt next to my father during those scary nights. It was Heidi's first chance to experience the closeness of a father after facing her storms without one. For the first time, her father was real to her—real enough to touch her—and that brought a joy and security no imaginary father ever could.

Question 1: Is God Real?

The first question those touched by the pain of life must face is this: Is God real? Is he as close as the father who held my hand during those thunderstorms? Is there a God in heaven who wants to be a father to us as much I want to be a father to Heidi?

When I sat immersed in despair at that California church, I was desperate to know: Was there actually a God who was paying attention to me? When I knelt down, the answer came in a way I never would have expected. But I knew God himself had given me his response.

What caused me to ask this question? It was the distress I was producing for others—Heidi, Holly, my roommates, my parents—and the distress I was feeling myself. I can wish now that the answer had come earlier, sparing all of us the anguish. But the truth is, before the pain, I wasn't asking this question. So do I regret the heartache? Yes—for me and for everyone affected by my choices. But I don't regret the fact that my pain ultimately propelled me to the point of asking whether God is real.

When I was telling the church about Heidi, I mentioned that the string of events leading to my meeting with Holly's husband could only be a miracle. I have heard over the years many accounts of so-called miracles that, upon close examination, have turned out to be more wishful thinking than anything. Yet I have also personally witnessed bona fide miracles that few would dispute.

I once made an offhand remark that someone should calculate the odds of that "chance" encounter at my parents' door. To my surprise, someone took me up on my challenge. A few days later, he handed me a note. "Being a mathematician by training," it read, "I just couldn't pass up the chance to run the odds on your meeting to see how it comes out." He calculated the likelihood of this occurring merely by chance by multiplying the separate odds of each factor involved. The answer: 1 in 500 billion. "The results are mind bending, to say the least," the mathematician concluded. "If any skeptics doubt that God was in this thing, I would defy them to explain these odds."

Of course, I would never claim these mathematical calculations provide empirical proof of the existence of God. But I have yet to hear a more convincing explanation than mine, that a God in heaven heard my pleas and personally arranged circumstances to bring about a restoration.

Question 2: Does God Care?

My conversations about the Heidi story have given me the opportunity to observe a variety of ways people respond to adversity. "My son has Down's syndrome," one woman told me. "It has caused me a lot of bitterness. I don't go to church anymore."

"God was really nice to you," another person told me. "But my mother died when I was a child, and I don't understand why God did that to me."

One girl told me she had been sexually abused when she was young and that her bitterness left an insurmountable barrier between her and her father. As we talked this over, I asked if she was angry with God. "I don't have any problem with God," she replied. "It's my father I have the problem with."

I didn't think it was quite that simple. "Do you believe that God was present while you were being abused?" I asked. She thought for a minute, then acknowledged he must have been. "Could he have stopped it?" I asked. "Couldn't he have given your father a heart attack?"

Again she paused. "I guess he can do whatever he wants," she said, "but for some reason he didn't stop it." Her face looked a bit troubled. This girl hesitated to blame God for the abuse she had suffered. But she had to reconcile the fact that he had the power to intervene in her catastrophe, yet he chose to allow it to happen.

Heidi faced the same dilemma. She had a father out there somewhere for seventeen years, but as much as she needed him, God refused to bring him into her life. "I hate you," she said to me during that emotion-laden encounter we had one night in New York. "I hate you, I hate you, I hate you. . . ." Her anger stemmed from my wrongdoing, and all I could do was to ask her to forgive me.

Feelings similar to those Heidi had can emerge when God doesn't live up to our expectations, whether they are appropriate or not. If he doesn't perform as we think an all-powerful God should, we end up disappointed, hurt, or angry with him. Some of us may not even consciously identify God as the one we're blaming.

This is what I began to suspect as I talked with the young woman who had been abused. "Maybe you need to forgive God," I told her, "for not being the protector you wanted him to be."

For some, God can seem like a passerby who witnesses a brutal crime yet refuses to become involved. If so, either he is unfeeling, callous, or unthinkably cruel. "How could a loving God allow such a thing?" we ask.

Perhaps it would be useful to explore three questions that can help us identify our concept of God.

What have you concluded about God's motives?

In that first serious clash with Heidi, I outraged her by my uninvited intrusion into her social life. As far as she was concerned, I had seized a position of parental authority she was not willing to surrender. As we talked, I assured her that some day she would realize my intentions were good. She had drawn the wrong conclusion about my motives. That's not unusual for children. How often does a son or daughter accuse his parents of cruelty when he or she simply does not comprehend the reason for their actions?

In the same way, a child has little idea how much delight a parent finds in the child's happiness. When I was playing baseball, I remember once thinking it must be sad for my dad to be stuck in the stands. "He would probably love to be out here himself," I thought. It wasn't until I had children that I realized my father probably was getting more satisfaction in the bleachers than I was on the mound. Like most kids, I didn't spend much time considering what my dad was thinking or feeling. The primary thing I was tuned into was whether or not he was giving me what I wanted. But as I got older and spent more time observing him, listening to him, and understanding his perspective, many of my impressions of him were clarified.

If you are suspicious of God's motives toward you, consider that his thoughts and feelings might be different from what you have assumed, his goals different from what you have surmised.

Can God feel your pain?

Most of us grew up with enough religious instruction to know God supposedly cares about us. "Jesus loves me, this I know," the song goes, "for the Bible tells me so." Childhood images contribute to our concept of God: a ceramic figurine glued to a miniature manger or a white-bearded grandfather in a flowing robe—someone at least as nice as the Tooth Fairy. The superficial stereotypes of God we've been exposed to since childhood seem to have little capacity to feel anything, much less experience the kind of pain we do.

The Bible paints a much different picture. Think about the life Jesus led. Was it one of privilege, insulated from hardship? Was he somehow able to walk in a protective bubble that shielded him from brutality or anguish?

The hotel clerk on duty that first Christmas Eve did not pull out the key to the presidential suite when the couple from Bethlehem showed up. All he could offer them was an animal's stall.

Jesus knew the struggle of poverty growing up in a working class home. He knew what it was to suffer loss; when his friend Lazarus died, Jesus was overcome with grief and wept openly. He knew what it was to be misunderstood; he spoke clearly, but his opponents twisted his teachings and subjected him to relentless verbal abuse. He knew what it was to be betrayed; a friend in his inner circle turned on him. He knew what it was to be physically abused; Roman soldiers shredded his back with a whip, stabbed his side with a spear, jammed a ring of thorns through his scalp, hammered spikes through his wrists, and hung him from crossed timbers. With his lungs crushed by his own weight, he slowly suffocated.

The physical and emotional abuse drove him to the point of ultimate despair, where he uttered the question that erupts in our most difficult hour: "My God, my God, why have you forsaken me?"

Does this picture of Jesus seem to show an unfeeling God who would be impatient with our questions or unmoved by our hardships?

If you're being asked to deal with circumstances that don't seem fair and point you to a conclusion that God doesn't care, ask yourself this: Am I having to endure something that Jesus himself did not suffer?

Meanwhile, while Jesus was suffering on earth, his father in heaven looked on without intervening. Why didn't he rush in and stop the cruelty? Might it be that as horrifying as it was for the father, he chose to hold back because he could see beyond the boundaries of time? If so, what does he see?

When does your life end?

Someone facing heart surgery undoubtedly fears the pain ahead. He knows the surgeon will rip open his chest and maneuver a critical organ. After he awakens from the anesthetic, the patient will suffer through his recovery and carry a scar for the rest of his life. Why is that patient willing to endure the pain of a heart operation?—for the hope of better health and the postponement of death.

The only way I know to reconcile the discomfort of life is to broaden our perspective beyond the confines of our few years on earth. If what you see around you is all there is to life, then the best advice would be to avoid pain at all costs. There is no reason to suffer if it won't improve your life. But as the lyrics of the 1988 Olympic theme song, "One Moment in Time," put it, "I broke my heart for every gain. To taste the sweet, I faced the pain."

On a relatively short time frame—at most, maybe a hundred or so years on earth——we might not be able to see any benefit to our pain. But when our life here is viewed merely as a warm-up, it becomes much easier to see why God would permit our pain—if it can somehow influence our eternal condition. Through my adversity, I learned more about life than I would have without it. I was driven to the hope that, through my failures, God was going to shape me into the kind of person he wanted me to be, preparing me for eternity.

It is only with this eternal perspective that Heidi and I have been able to understand her entry into the world. If her birth resulted just from two people's foolish choices, then her life is horribly unfair. Why should she have had to pay the price for other people's errors?

Only from this point of view does it become clear that Heidi's birth was not a mistake. God makes decisions when it comes to birth and death; he opens and shuts the womb. Heidi was born for a purpose. God has used the trauma resulting from her entry into the world to direct both of us to the deeper questions of life, to help us understand himself. He allowed the necessary pain to accomplish something of lasting value, yet at the same time shielded her from much hardship that easily could have befallen her.

Question 3: So what's the point?

If you agree that life doesn't conclude with your funeral, what, then, will you carry beyond the grave? Someone else will fill the job you leave. Your bank account will pass on to your heirs. Your wardrobe will be readied for a Salvation Army pickup. So what about our lives is eternal?

I once took a group of high school students through an exercise that showed what they valued most in life. "Who would be afraid to go to hell?" I asked them. Several indicated they were not afraid, and that they were even anticipating the trip. When I asked why they thought it wouldn't be that bad, one said: "Because I'll be with my friends." They all nodded in agreement, with complete sincerity.

These teenagers, who unknowingly answered the question of what is eternal, were echoing the theme that has resounded through every generation. They were saying that what they value most is relationships—even if it means enduring the ultimate punishment.

Life's central theme

Agreement is nearly universal that relationship is our central human need. Our culture's art, literature, and music most often depict themes related to the joys of romance and friendship or the pain of loneliness or rejection.

Over the years of your life, what would you say has brought you the greatest joy? You've already read about some of my highlights: the joy of first seeing Heidi, her grasping my hand, hearing her call me "Dad." Now consider what has produced your greatest sorrow. For me, my separation from Heidi produced a profound sadness. If you're like the many other people whom I have asked these questions, your answers will show that your highest joys and deepest sorrows ultimately can be traced back to your relationships. Do you think it's safe to say relationship is what gives life meaning? This is the conclusion I've reached. Giving and receiving love is what God has in mind for us; that's what Jesus made the trip from heaven to tell us and show us.

Despite our ability to identify this deep human need, we don't seem very able to satisfy it, thus our loneliness, our anguish, our pain. The fact is, we live in a world where broken relationships are responsible for much of the damage in our lives, whether they're broken by something we've done, by an offense committed by someone else, or by some outside force.

Why do relationships break down? Why are healthy relationships so difficult?

The disease

The problem as I understand it is that we have all contracted a deadly disease that attacks relationships and makes perfect ones impossible. This condition is genetic and has spread through the entire human race. We have placed various labels on the symptoms. We say, "He's arrogant," "She's selfish," "He lied to me," "She betrayed me," "He ripped me off." But we all know these symptoms produce our pain. The disease that produces all of these symptoms God has identified as sin.

Most of us have an easier time diagnosing this disease in other people. But as we sort through the deeper questions of life, we'll have to determine whether we ourselves are infected as well. When you admit you are a carrier of this virus, you're basically saying you have done things to damage a relationship.

When God issued the Ten Commandments, he was not giving us a checklist of do's and don'ts that he would use to grade our performance. He was actually laying a foundation for healthy relationship. When you lie or steal, for example, God isn't upset because you broke a rule. He is upset because you damaged a relationship. Sin, however it emerges, is a relationship killer.

Musician Kris Kristofferson was interviewed about the drug and alcohol dependence that once controlled his life. He commented that the most damaging result of his habit was that it ruined his relationships. That was the wound that left the deepest scar on his life.

The antidote

When Heidi sat on that couch in my parents' house and vented her anger, I had to look her in the eye and admit I was guilty of not being a father to her. I had no excuse. The only hope for a restored relationship was for the innocent to forgive the guilty. Her choice relieved me. She forgave me and opened up her life to me. But I also wanted her to understand something else that night. Instead of seeing herself solely as a victim, I wanted to be sure she understood that she, too, had contracted the relationship disease. She, too, had wronged other people. She, too, had made choices to think and act in ways that produced grief for others. "I forgive you for those things," I told her.

"Let him who is without sin cast the first stone," Jesus said to the men preparing to stone the adulterous woman. No one is exempt from the relationship disease. Heidi began to understand that night both her need to forgive me and her need to ask God to forgive her. Only forgiveness can open the door to the restoration of relationship.

*H*OPE FOR RELATIONSHIP

Not long ago, tragedy tore into a family in our church. Their seven-year-old boy was struck by a car in front of their house. The child remained unconscious, and I joined the family in the intensive care unit, watching him fight for his life. Without prompting, a network of friends immediately had closed in to provide a safety net of comfort and support. As the mother and father stood at his bedside, several people waited with them around the clock. Others filled in the gap to console and care for their other two children, provide the family with meals, and handle practical household matters that needed attention. In the midst of the anguish of that vigil, they were also deeply moved by the outpouring of love.

The next Sunday as I stood before our congregation, I posed a question that had been on my mind since the accident. I asked what choice they would make if faced with two options, having a life free of pain but absent of love or having a life vulnerable to tragedy and heartache but one in which they would experience love.

This was the choice God faced. He is powerful enough to blot out pain; but he made a world where the opportunity to love also brought the possibility of sorrow.

A few weeks after I spoke with the congregation, a woman who had pondered these two options wrote me this letter:

> *I want to thank you for the short exhortation you gave a few weeks ago, posing the question of whether we would*

choose a life without love in order to avoid pain or a life with pain in order to love.

Back in my early teens, I reacted to the pain, bitterness, and anger I saw and felt by making a vow to a God I didn't know that I would never let myself be made vulnerable by love. But in the last months, God has lovingly forced me to face the pain I've run from for years, a foul cesspool of fear.

I don't know exactly what happened, but something has been resolved, and I'm no longer afraid of the pain, no longer afraid to love. Your exhortation clarified some of that and helped seal it in my heart.

Like many of us, this young woman's response to pain, even the prospect of it, was to cut herself off from love. We're tempted to try this apparent solution when the pangs of guilt, or the feelings of loneliness, humiliation, or loss come without invitation. They overtake us when we're lying in bed at night, taking a walk, listening to a particular song, or passing through holiday seasons. We can try to pretend the hurt isn't there. But this is like an adult trying to cover up with a baby blanket; no matter how tightly he tries to curl up, he's still exposed.

Rather than shrink back from possible hardship, I want to encourage you: Don't be afraid of life. Don't be afraid of the circumstances that might come your way. They are under the control of a loving God to whom you can safely yield yourself.

Our relationship with our creator—someone who knows infinitely more than we do—requires that we let go of our demand for answers to all our questions. God wants us to love him, and love does not insist on a full explanation. Hope for relationship with God lies in the realm of faith more than reason—faith that there is a God who is determined to produce something in us of eternal value and will go to any length to bring that to pass. Though this perspective eliminates the prospect of escaping the dangers of living, we can be confident God's ultimate goal for us is more valuable than our physical and emotional safety.

Job is a character in the Bible who is famous for his patience; he was willing to wait a lifetime to understand why God was allowing circumstances to torment him. Meanwhile, Job's so-called "comforters" were those who insisted on answers. They offered well thought out but inadequate explanations of how God was dealing with Job.

But Job never gave up hope. He wrestled with God in the midst of his suffering, but when the answers didn't come, he decided to trust God anyway. Job lost his health, his family, his possessions, his comfort. But his hope gained him a greater capacity to love and trust God.

If you approach God with this trust, then you can also enter a life of relationship with other people without fearing the possible pain. With this trust, you can survive abuses, offenses, failures. What you can't survive is the absence of love.

So as you confront the sorrows of your life, I cannot promise that the raw places can be healed immediately. But I do feel I have something substantial to offer as you walk through your emotional combat zones—hope that restoration is possible in a world ruled not by bitterness and sorrow, but a place where love links people with God and one another.

Looking back at the events of the past twenty years, I would never have wished my suffering on myself or anyone else, yet I can clearly see the hand of God. The events I have recounted in this book changed me; they changed my values, my goals, my perspectives. They brought me unhappiness, but I learned more about love and relationship than if they had never transpired.

"For I know the plans I have for you," declares the Lord, "plans to prosper you and not to harm you, plans to give you hope and a future."
— Jeremiah 29:11

APPENDIX:
THE FAMILY ALBUM

Mother and daughter celebrate Heidi's second birthday.

One of Holly and Heidi's regular outings to feed ducks.

Heidi atop a cannon in Gettysburg during a special day with Mom.

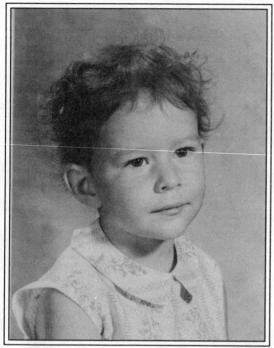

At three-years-old, a
portrait for the
family album.

Getting down to
business with Santa
Claus.

A favorite photo of
mother and
daughter.

**Country
life:
chasing
butterflies
with pet
cat Frigga
Loki.**

**Heidi,
15, at the
Lilly
Pond
Festival.**

**A junior
in high
school.**

Heidi and Joe; their first day together.

Heidi introduces Joe to some people who befriended her, the Joe Dorr family.

An emotional moment as Joe introduces Heidi to his church family.

The church greets Heidi, Holly, and Joe's family.

Initiated into
the joys of
family life
with Dawn,
Jodi, and Joy.

Quiet time
between
brother and
sister.

Heidi's new grandparents: Joe Sr. and Connie.

Joe with his sister Marybeth and his brother John.

Heidi and Marybeth under the magnolia tree.

Look what
Heidi got for
Christmas.

Getting
comfortable
in her new
role.

Joe Sr. with the grandkids on Long Island.

A happy conclusion.

Two
lives...
separate...
no more.

Also from Cityhill . . .

Restoration In The Church by Terry Virgo
A fresh look at the new generation of churches that challenge the notion of the church as a cold, uninviting monument.

Living God's Way by Arthur Wallis
A study manual for understanding basic concepts of the Christian life.

On To Maturity by Arthur Wallis
An insightful and practical study course applying Bible truths to the challenges we face every day.

The Radical Christian by Arthur Wallis
A tough message showing what can be expected when one steps beyond the safe limits of traditional religion.

China Miracle by Arthur Wallis
A fast-moving account of the church in China, yesterday and today.

In The Day of Thy Power by Arthur Wallis
A picture of how God moves in Scripture and in history.

Queen Take Your Throne by Eileen Wallis
Drawing from the life of Queen Esther, this set of sixteen Bible studies offers sensible answers for today's woman.

Pocket Principles for Leaders by Costa Deir
Designed to fit the businessman's inside coat pocket, each book in this set contains concise capsules of wisdom for today's leaders.

Lives In Focus edited by Richard Myhre
Fourteen profiles of ordinary people learning of struggle and strength.

Check your local bookstore or order direct from:
Cityhill Publishing,
4600 Christian Fellowship Road
Columbia, MO 65203

Call Cityhill's toll-free order line: 1-800-733-8093